The Bridge of Stars

The Bridge of Stars

365 Prayers, Blessings and Meditations
from around the World

Foreword by His Holiness the Dalai Lama

General Editor: Marcus Braybrooke

dbp

DUNCAN BAIRD PUBLISHERS

LONDON

Contents

The Bridge of Stars
Marcus Braybrooke

First published in the United Kingdom and Ireland in 2001 by
Duncan Baird Publishers Ltd
Sixth Floor
Castle House
75–76 Wells Street
London W1T 3QH

Conceived, created and designed by Duncan Baird Publishers

Editorial Consultant: Oliver Baird
Managing Editor: Judy Barratt
Editor: Hanne Bewernick
Managing Designer: Manisha Patel
Designer: Suzanne Tuhrim
Picture Researcher: Cee Weston-Baker

British Library Cataloguing-in-Publication Data:
A CIP record for this book is available from the British Library.

ISBN: 1-903296-27-7

10 9 8 7 6 5 4 3 2 1

Typeset in Phaistos and Gill Sans
Colour reproduction by Colourscan, Singapore
Printed and bound in Singapore by Imago

NOTES
Abbreviations used throughout this book:
CE Common Era (the equivalent of AD)
BCE Before the Common Era (the equivalent of BC)
b. Born
d. Died

Foreword

When I meet people in different parts of the world, I am always reminded that we are all basically alike. Maybe we wear different clothes, our skin is of a different colour, or we speak different languages. These are only superficial differences; basically, we are the same human beings. Our basic sameness makes it possible for us to understand each other and to develop friendship and closeness.

As human beings, we all want to be happy and to avoid suffering. In my limited experience, if we are to achieve this, it is immensely valuable to be able to cultivate and maintain a positive state of mind. In the Buddhist tradition to which I belong, one of the most effective means of doing so is to engage in meditation. Now, meditation can sometimes mean sitting in a formal posture and stilling the mind, but primarily it means continuously familiarizing ourselves with positive thoughts.

All religions make the betterment of humanity their main concern. Therefore, it gives me great pleasure to introduce this book, *The Bridge of Stars*, a collection of prayers from a wide range of places and times. I believe that the core advice that most of these prayers contain is that we should each make our lives as meaningful as possible.

With a prayer to reflect on every day of the year, I trust that readers will find some inspiration in this book to develop in themselves that warm-hearted peace of mind that is the key to enduring happiness.

Dalai Lama

March 5, 2001

★

All our days and nights

On rising

1 The beauty we love

Today, like every day,

we wake up hollow and frightened.

Don't open the door to the study and begin reading.

Reach for a musical instrument.

Let the beauty we love be what we do.

There are hundreds of ways to kneel and kiss the ground.

Jalil al–Din Rumi (1207–73), Persia

2 Awakening

O Lord

Open our eyes to your Presence

Open our minds to your grace

Open our lips to your praises

Open our hearts to your love

Open our lives to your healing

And be found among us.

Modern prayer by David Adam, from Tides and
Seasons, *England*

3 Mornings in heaven

Your enjoyment of the world is never right

until every morning you awake in heaven, see

yourself in God's palace, and look upon the

skies and the Earth and the air as celestial joys,

having such a loving regard of all these

as if you were among the angels.

Thomas Traherne (1637–74), England

4 Give thanks

When you arise in the morning, give

thanks for the morning light.

Give thanks for your life and your strength.

Give thanks for your food

and give thanks for the joy of living.

And if you see no reason for giving thanks,

rest assured that the fault is in yourself.

Chief Tecumseh of the Shawnee Nation (d.1813), USA

5 An offering of time

Lord, I have time,

I have plenty of time,

All the time that you give me,

The years of my life,

The days of my years,

The hours of my days,

They are all mine.

Mine to fill, quietly, calmly,

But to fill completely up to the brim,

To offer them to you.

Michel Quoist (b.1921), France

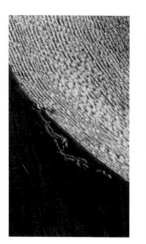

6 You have watched over me

Living Lord, you have watched over me, and put your hand on my head, during the long, dark hours of night. Your holy angels have protected me from all harm and pain. To you, Lord, I owe life itself. Continue to watch over me and bless me during the hours of day.

Jacob Boehme (1575–1624), Germany

7 The experiment

Morning means just Risk—to the Lover—

Just revelation—to the Beloved

Epicures—date a Breakfast—by it

Brides—an Apocalypse—

Worlds—a Flood—

Faint-going Lives—Their Lapse from Sighing—

Faith—The Experiment of Our Lord—

Emily Dickinson (1830–86), USA

Promise of morning

8 Take time

Take time to think …

It is the source of power.

Take time to play …

It is the secret of perpetual youth.

Take time to laugh …

It is the music of the soul.

Take time to pray …

It is the greatest power on Earth.

Words written on the wall of the Missionaries of Charity children's home, Calcutta, India

9 Dawn flowers

How I long to see

among dawn flowers

the face of God.

Basho (1644–94), Japan

10 The right moment

There is only one moment in time

when it is essential to awaken.

That moment is now.

The Buddha (c.563–c.483BCE), India

11 Joyful rising

My Lord, what a morning, my Lord, what a morning,

My Lord, what a morning, when the stars begin to fall!

Charles Albert Tindley (1851–1933), USA

12 Be not afraid of my body

As Adam early in the morning,

walking forth from the bower refresh'd with sleep

Behold me where I pass, hear my voice approach,

Touch me, touch the palm of your hand to my body as I pass,

Be not afraid of my body.

Walt Whitman (1819–92), USA

13 The windowsill of heaven

Every morning lean your arms awhile upon the

windowsill of heaven and gaze upon the Lord.

Then with the vision in your heart, turn strong

to meet your day.

Modern prayer by Thomas Blake

14 Litany

I hold the splendid daylight in my hands

Inwardly grateful for a lovely day.

Thank you life.

Daylight like a fine fan spread from my hands

Daylight like scarlet poinsettia

Daylight like yellow cassia flowers

Daylight like clean water

Daylight like green cacti

Daylight like sea sparkling with white horses

Daylight like sunstrained blue sky

Daylight like tropic hills

Daylight like a sacrament in my hands.

Amen.

George Campbell (b.1916), Jamaica

15 Stepping out to awareness

When I step out,

> the world assembles itself around me

like my awareness of being who I am,

> like my belief in the Divine.

Modern prayer from Stockholm, Sweden

16 The day ahead

Who can tell what a day might bring? Therefore, gracious God, cause me to live every day as if it were to be my last, for I know not but that it may be such. Cause me to live now as I shall wish I had done when I come to die.

Thomas à Kempis (1379/80–1471), Germany

Greetings and partings

17 Well met!

Good day, my friend. This chance encounter

augurs well for my contentment. I thank

God that He should bring you across my path.

I was hurrying. It is fit that I slow down to

luxuriate in your wisdom and probity.

Greeting from Salem (19th century), USA

18 Traveler's blessing

May the road rise to meet you.

May the wind be always at your back.

May the sun shine warm upon your face.

May the rains fall softly upon your fields.

Until we meet again

May God hold you in the hollow of his hand.

Traditional Gaelic blessing

19   Wisdom, voice, bounty

Wisdom of serpent be yours,

Wisdom of raven be yours,

Wisdom of valiant eagle.

Voice of swan be yours,

Voice of honey be yours,

Voice of the son of the stars.

Bounty of sea be yours,

Bounty of land be yours,

Bounty of the Father of Heaven.

Traditional Celtic blessing

20 In God's hands

In your journeys to and fro

    God direct you;

In your happiness and pleasure

    God bless you;

In care, anxiety or trouble

    God sustain you;

In peril and in danger

    God protect you.

Archbishop Timothy Olufosoye (1918–92), Nigeria

21 Deep peace

Deep peace of the running waves to you,

Deep peace of the flowing air to you,

Deep peace of the quiet earth to you,

Deep peace of the shining stars to you,

Deep peace of the shades of night to you,

Moon and stars always giving light to you.

Traditional Gaelic blessing

22 Pilgrimage

Give me my scallop-shell of quiet,

My staff of faith to walk upon,

My scrip of joy, immortal diet,

My bottle of salvation,

My gown of glory, hope's true gage;

And thus I'll take my pilgrimage.

Sir Walter Raleigh (1552–1618), England
(scrip: *certificate* / gage: *measure*)

Gifts of the table

23 At the table

The table is set with precious food.

We sit and wait, Jesus,

in expectation of the moment

when we eat and drink with you.

Modern prayer from Nigeria

24 A hungry boy and girl

Let us pause for a moment before we sit down to eat.

Before we satisfy our hunger,

let us wait for a little girl in the famine-stricken

desert to take her first mouthful of her first meal

for a week.

Let us pause for a moment before we sit down to eat.

Before we satisfy our hunger,

let us wait for a little boy in the famine-stricken

mountains to take his first mouthful of his first meal

for a week.

Modern prayer from Los Angeles, USA

25 Goodness of water

The highest good is like that of the water.

The goodness of water is that it benefits

the ten thousand creatures, yet itself does

not scramble, but is content with the places

that all men disdain.

Lao-tzu (c.604–c.531 BCE), China

26 Via sun and rain

Give thanks for the farmers, and for everyone in the

long chain from soil to mouth via sun and rain.

Give thanks for the plenty in our lives.

Let every mouthful remind us of the privilege of

being alive and more-than-adequately fed,

of being among like-minded souls, and sharing a

wholesome, flavorsome meal.

Modern prayer from Sicily, Italy

27 Bless our meal

Bless our meal, dear Lord,

Bless us all, each one of us,

And let us find among pain and joy

That you have lit your peace in our home.

J.I. Bondesen (1844–1911), Denmark

28 God provides

You cause the grass to grow for the cattle,

    and plants for people to use,

to bring forth food from the earth,

    and wine to gladden the human heart,

oil to make the face shine,

    and bread to strengthen the human heart.

Psalms 104:14–15

A good day's work

29 Song for fine weather

O Good Sun,

Look you down upon us:

Shine, shine on us, O Sun,

Gather up the clouds, wet, black, under your arms—

That the rains may cease to fall.

Because your friends are all here on the beach

Ready to go fishing—

Ready for the hunt.

Therefore look kindly on us, O Good Sun!

Give us peace within our tribe

And with all our enemies.

Again, again we call—

Hear us, hear us, O Good Sun!

Indian Haida song, Canada

30 On a busy day

O Lord, You know how busy I must be this day.

If I forget You, do not forget me.

Jacob Astley (1579–1652), England

★

31 One thing at a time

As I prepare to go about my work today,

    may my intention to live in your present moment

    be the pattern for this day and my life.

With your help, may I forever do

    only one thing at a time—

    always in communion with you, my Beloved,

    with all my heart and mind and soul.

Modern prayer by Edward Hays, USA

★

32 Our task

The fact that our task is exactly as large as

our life makes it appear infinite.

Franz Kafka (1883–1924), Czechoslovakia

33 An active life

God give me work

Till my life shall end

And life

Till my work is done.

Epitaph, Winifred Holtby (1898–1935), England

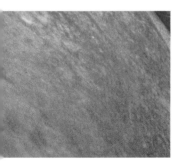

34 The rosary

My task ahead is like a rosary.

In the hours this work will take,
    miracles will happen unobserved
    within my body and mind.
My spirit will grow in maturity.
My love for humankind will make
    some new acquaintances.
I will savor each second,
    lay down each minute
    carefully and joyously,
    a brick in the temple of my being.

My task ahead is like a rosary.

Modern prayer from Madrid, Spain

As evening falls

35 Around the fire

May the Sacred Three

Save,

Shield,

Surround,

The hearth,

The house,

The household,

This eve,

This night,

Oh! this eve,

This night,

And every night,

Each single night.

Amen.

Traditional Celtic blessing to celebrate Samhain, the Celtic new year (November 1st)

36 A beauteous evening

It is a beauteous evening, calm and free,

The holy time is quiet as a Nun

Breathless with adoration; the broad sun

Is sinking down in its tranquillity;

The gentleness of heaven broods o'er the Sea:

Listen! the mighty Being is awake,

And doth with his eternal motion make

A sound like thunder—everlastingly.

From a poem by William Wordsworth (1770–1850), England

37 Sunset prayer

All our problems

We send to the Cross of Christ.

All our difficulties

We send to the Cross of Christ.

All the devil's works

We send to the Cross of Christ.

All our hopes

We set on the Risen Son.

From the Kenyan Revised Liturgy for
Holy Communion, 1987

38 Evening affirmation

—Night is drawing nigh—

For all that has been—Thanks!

For all that shall be—Yes!

Dag Hammarskjöld (1905–61), Sweden

39 Sound of evening

Dying cricket—

how full of

life, his song.

Basho (1644–94), Japan

40 Evening prayer

When I see the moon in the night sky

I speak my evening prayer:

Praise be to the Being of Life,

For His kindness and His goodness.

After a traditional Celtic prayer

41 Dews of quietness

Drop your still dews of quietness,

Till all our striving cease;

Take from our souls the strain and stress,

And let our ordered lives confess

The beauty of your peace.

John Greenleaf Whittier (1807–92), USA

42 Winding down

Slow me down, Lord!

Ease the pounding of my heart by the

quieting of my mind.

Steady my hurried pace with a vision of the

eternal reach of time.

Give me, after the confusion of the day, the

calmness of the everlasting rills.

Break the tensions of my nerves and muscles

with the soothing music of the singing

streams that live in my memory.

Modern prayer by Orin L. Crain, USA

Time for sleep

43 Bedtime prayer

The sun has disappeared.

I have switched off the light,

And my wife and children are asleep.

The animals in the forest are full of fear,

And so are the people on their mats.

They prefer the day with your sun

To the night.

But I still know that your moon is there,

And your eyes and also your hands.

Thus I am not afraid.

This day again

You led us wonderfully.

Everybody went to his mat

Satisfied and full.

Renew us during our sleep,

That in the morning we may come afresh

   to our daily jobs.

Be with our brothers far away in Asia

Who may be getting up now. Amen.

Prayer of a young Christian, Ghana

44 The great hymn of night

I listen to the rush of wind from the mountain and the valley

and feel my soul joining in like a string in the great hymn.

Then dusk covers the tracks of my dreams.

I fall asleep on my bed of moss.

All is quiet.

Knut Hamsun (1859–1952), Norway

45 Dream rendezvous

When evening comes

I will leave the door open beforehand

   and then wait

For him who said he would come

To meet me in my dreams.

Yakamochi (d.785CE), Japan

46 Song of evening

Stay with us when the day wanes,

dear God our Father!

Stay with us when the darkness wells

out of the locks of night!

Stay with us, and we will dream

about the peace of angel children.

Your spirit through heavenly streams

will rush down to us.

B.S. Ingemann (1789–1862), Denmark

47 The wings of sleep

O Lord our God, King of the Universe.

Let the wings of sleep fall upon my eyes, and

   upon my eyelids.

O blessed One,

Let me lie down in peace, and rise in peace.

Into Your hand I entrust my spirit.

Adapted from a Jewish prayer

48 Night vigil

Watch, dear Lord,

with those who wake, or watch, or weep tonight,

and give your angels charge over those who sleep.

Tend your sick ones, O Lord Christ,

rest your weary ones.

Bless your dying ones.

Soothe your suffering ones.

Pity your afflicted ones.

Shield your joyous ones.

And all for your love's sake,

Amen.

St Augustine of Hippo (354–430), North Africa

49 Song of light

Lord Jesus, Son of God,

This night as every night

All life, all joy comes from you;

The stars and planets,

And each soft glowing hue,

Reflect the glory of your light.

After a 2nd-century prayer from Egypt

50 Hymn to night

Night, shield us from the wolf and thief.

Throughout your hours let there be calm.

Pitch dark has brought a shroud for me.

Dawn, drive it, like my debts, away.

Child of Day, to you, as to a calf,

My hymn is offered.

From the Rig Veda *(c.1500–c.1000BCE), India*

51 Prayer by moonshine

The cold night winds sigh,

My eyes are heavy with sleep.

Give me, O God, your peace.

Look to my slumber in your mercy

And comfort me in my sorrow

And comfort my sick neighbor too.

Matthias Claudius (1740–1815), from "The Moon Has Risen", Germany

52 Wanderer's nightsong

Over the hill-tops

Is peace,

In the tree-tops

You feel

Hardly a breath.

The little birds are silent in the forest:

Just wait; soon

You too shall be at rest.

Johann Wolfgang Goethe (1749–1832), Germany

53 In the evening

The sun has set,

I sit and rest my weary body,

   and think of you.

Give my body peace.

Let my legs and arms stop aching.

Let my head stop thinking.

Let me sleep in your arms.

Adapted from a Dinka prayer, Sudan

The revolving year

Living in nature

54 Splendid hues

Will you not open your heart to know

What rainbows teach, and sunsets show?

Ralph Waldo Emerson (1803–82), USA

55 Everywhere at hand

And look into space; you shall see Him

walking in the cloud,

Outstretching his arms in the lightning

and descending in rain.

You shall see him smiling in flowers,

Then rising and waving his hands in trees.

Kahlil Gibran (1883–1931), from The Prophet,
Lebanon

56 Nature's sweetness

May the wind blow sweetness,

The rivers flow sweetness,

The herbs grow sweetness,

For the Man of Truth!

Sweet be the night,

Sweet the dawn,

Sweet be Earth's fragrance,

Sweet Father Heaven!

May the tree afford us sweetness,

The sun shine sweetness,

Our cows yield sweetness—

Milk in plenty!

From the Rig Veda (c.1500–c.1000BCE), India

57 Druid song

I am the wind on the sea.

I am the wave of the sea.

I am the bull of seven battles.

I am the eagle on the rock.

I am a flash from the sun.

I am the most beautiful of plants.

I am a strong wild boar.

I am a salmon in the water.

I am a lake in the plain.

I am the word of knowledge.

I am the head of the spear in battle.

I am the God that puts fire in the head.

Who spreads light in the gathering on the hills?

Who can tell the ages of the moon?

Who can tell the place where the sun rests?

Druid Amergin (c.600BCE), Ireland

58 Behold

Above, above

all birds in air

Below, below

all earth's flowers

Inland, inland

all forest trees

Seaward, seaward

all ocean fish

Sing out and say

again the refrain:

Behold this lovely world.

*Anonymous (19th century),
Hawaii,* USA

59 Song of beauty

The voice that beautifies the land!

The voice above,

The voice of the thunder,

Among the dark clouds

Again and again it sounds,

The voice that beautifies the land.

The voice that beautifies the land!

The voice below,

The voice of the grasshopper,

Among the flowers and grasses

Again and again it sounds,

The voice that beautifies the land.

Native American Navajo song, USA

60 Song of the sky loom

O our Mother the Earth, O our Father the Sky,

Your children are we, and with tired backs

We bring you the gifts you love.

Then weave for us a garment of brightness;

May the warp be the white light of morning,

May the weft be the red light of evening,

May the fringes be the falling rain,

May the border be the standing rainbow.

So weave for us a garment of brightness,

That we may walk fittingly where birds sing,

That we may walk fittingly where grass is green,

O our Mother the Earth, O our Father the Sky.

Tewa Indian prayer (19th century), USA

61 Drinking the shadows

I am a shadow far from dark villages.

I drank God's silence

Out of the deep well of the trees.

Georg Trakl (1887–1914), from De Profundis, *Austria*

62 Prayer for the animals

For those, O Lord,

the humble beasts,

that bear with us

the burden and heat of the day,

and offer their guileless lives

for the well-being of humankind;

and for the wild creatures,

whom You have made

wise, strong and beautiful,

we supplicate for them

Your great tenderness of heart,

for You have promised to save

both human and beast,

and great is Your loving kindness,

O Master,

Savior of the world.

*St Basil the Great, Bishop of Caesarea (329–379),
Cappadocia*

63 Earthsong

Awake, O north wind,

and come, O south wind!

Blow upon my garden

that its fragrance may be wafted abroad.

Let my beloved come to his garden,

and eat its choicest fruits.

Song of Solomon 4:16

64 Hymn to Aten

All cattle rest upon their pastures,

The trees and the plants flourish,

The birds flutter in their marshes,

Their wings uplifted in adoration to you.

All the sheep dance upon their feet,

All winged things fly,

They live when you have shone upon them.

The boats sail upstream and downstream alike.

Every highway is open because you dawn.

The fish in the river leap up before you.

Your rays are in the midst of the great

green sea.

Pharaoh Akhenaten (1353–36BCE), Egypt

65 The life of all that lives

I am the taste of water.

I am the light of the Sun and the Moon.

I am the original fragrance of the Earth.

I am the heat in fire.

I am the life of all that lives.

Of lights I am the radiant Sun.

Among stars I am the Moon.

Of bodies of water I am the ocean.

Of immovable things I am the Himalayas.

Of trees I am the banyan-tree.

Of weapons I am the thunderbolt.

Among beasts I am the lion.

Of purifiers I am the wind.

Of fishes I am the shark.

Of flowing rivers I am the Ganges.

Of seasons I am flower-bearing spring.

Of secret things I am silence.

Know that all opulent, beautiful and

glorious creations spring from but a spark

of my splendor.

From the Bhagavad Gita (1st–2nd century), India

Spring: a time of growth

66 Song of awakening

Teach me, O glorious Spring,

the lesson that nothing dies completely.

At the death of my body help me to know

that I have not entered an endless winter,

but simply a stage in the unfolding mystery

whose name is Life.

On this feast of the spring equinox

may I taste with delight

the freshness and vitality of new birth

and come forth from the womb of winter

youthful with hope

and fully alive

in the presence of my God.

Modern prayer by Edward Hays, USA

67 Spring morning

Spring—through

morning mist,

what mountain's there?

Basho (1644–94), Japan

68 Prayer for rain

Give life to the grass

by sending us rain.

Give life to our earth

by sending us rain.

Give life to our crops

by sending us rain.

Give life to our children

by sending us rain.

Dinka prayer, Sudan

69 The land awakens

Awake, the land is scattered with light, and see;

Uncanopied sleep is flying from field and tree:

And blossoming boughs of April in laughter shake,

Awake, O heart, to be loved, awake, awake!

Robert Bridges (1844–1930), from "Awake", England

70 Abundant love

My love

is like the grasses

hidden in the deep mountain:

though its abundance increases,

nobody knows.

Ono No Yoshiki (d.902CE), Japan

71 Winter is past

For now winter is past,

    the rain is over and gone.

The flowers appear on the earth;

    the time of singing has come,

and the voice of the turtledove

    is heard in our land.

Song of Solomon 2:11–12

72 Spring

Nothing is so beautiful as Spring—

    When weeds, in wheels, shoot long and lovely and lush;

    Thrush's eggs look little low heavens, and thrush

Through the echoing timber does so rinse and wring

The ear, it strikes like lightnings to hear him sing;

    The glassy peartree leaves and blooms, they brush

    The descending blue; that blue is all in a rush

With richness; the racing lambs too have fair their fling.

What is all this juice and all this joy?

    A strain of the earth's sweet being in the beginning

In Eden garden.

Gerard Manley Hopkins (1844–89), from "Spring", England

Summer: a time of fullness

73 In residence

In summer migrant birds arrive from the south.

If I am lucky I will see my first swallow

flying in from the sea.

But more likely, I will suddenly be aware that

these swallows have been wheeling

overhead for days.

At any moment we might wake to the fact that

God has entered our lives.

Only rarely do we see him taking up residence.

Modern prayer from England

74 Moon

On this summer night

All the household lies asleep,

And in the doorway,

For once open after dark,

Stands the moon, brilliant, cloudless.

Jusammi Chikako (c.1300), Japan

75 A prayer of the heart

The prayer of the heart is the source

of all good, refreshing

the soul as if it were a garden.

St Gregory of Sinai (d.1360), Egypt

76 Shade and sun

The house of God

   shades us from the blazing sun of the ego—

Outside we shrivel in error.

Modern prayer from New Mexico, USA

77 Waking on a summer morning

Break out from your slumber, throw off your sorrow.

Ah, what you suffered, it was only a dream.

Climb the hill, and see how morning

Borders the night sky with purple.

The stars grow pale; full of joy and reverence

The singing lark articulates the morning prayer,

The shadows flee from the face of the sun,

Who begins her restless march of triumph.

Theodor Fontane (1819–98), Germany

78 The fruitful tree

Blessed are those who trust in the Lord,

    whose trust is in the Lord.

They shall be like a tree planted by water,

    sending out its roots by a stream.

It shall not fear when heat comes,

    and its leaves shall stay green;

In the year of drought it is not anxious,

    and does not cease to bear fruit.

Jeremiah 17:7–8

Autumn: a time of gathering

79 Turn my soil

Turn over

Gently

My dry, cracked soil.

Just a little,

Let it breathe

In the cooling air of autumn

And then be watered

By Your life-giving rain.

Kathy Keay (d.1994), England

80 Autumn day

Lord: it is time. The summer was enormous.

Lay down your shadow on the sundials,

And on the meadows set the winds free.

Command the last fruits to fullness;

Grant them two more southerly days,

Press them toward perfection and chase

The last sweetness into the heavy wine.

Rainer Maria Rilke (1875–1926), Austria

81 Autumn forest

Of the turbid pool that lies in the autumn forest,

Of the moon that descends the steeps of the soughing twilight,

Toss, sparkles of day and dusk—toss on the black stems that decay in the muck,

Toss to the moaning gibberish of the dry limbs.

I ascend from the moon, I ascend from the night,

I perceive that the ghastly glimmer is noonday sunbeams reflected,

And debouch to the steady and central from the offspring great or small.

Walt Whitman (1819–92), from "Song of Myself", USA

82 Psalm of contentment

O sacred season of Autumn, be my teacher,

   for I wish to learn the virtue of contentment.

As I gaze upon your full-colored beauty,

   I sense all about you

   an at-homeness with your amber riches.

Modern prayer by Edward Hays, USA

83   The color of autumn

Early autumn—

rice fields, ocean,

one green.

Basho (1644–94), Japan

84   A misty morning

I saw old Autumn in the misty morn

Stand shadowless like Silence, listening

To silence.

Thomas Hood (1799–1845), from "Autumn",
England

85 Green to brown

Autumn withdraws summer's green

back into its wardrobe—

let us hope that green suits us just as much next year.

Modern haiku from Halifax, Canada

Winter: a time of reflection

86 Doubts melt like snow

An overnight sprinkling of snow—

our doubts, chased away by morning

as faith climbs even wintry skies.

Modern haiku from Paris, France

87 Lighten my darkness

You well of light from which my soul drank

deeply in the season of roses,

You shine forth from my inner day,

when darkness keeps me imprisoned.

J.S. Welhaven (1807–73), Norway

88 Winter fields

Winter under cultivation

Is as arable as spring.

Emily Dickinson (1830–86), USA

89 Pure and clear

Make Thou my spirit pure and clear

As are the frosty skies,

Or this first snowdrop of the year

That in my bosom lies.

John Keats (1795–1821), England

90 Darkness

When it is dark enough you can

see the stars.

Charles A. Beard (1874–1948), USA

91 The hearth

Around the fire we friends in a group

stretch out our arms and warm our hands.

All of us take great comfort from these coals.

Beyond the window a blizzard swirls in the night.

These snowflakes are each of them unique,

like fingerprints, or souls.

Modern meditation from St Petersburg, Russia

92 Bare boughs

In Winter the bare boughs that seem to sleep

Work covertly, preparing for their Spring.

Jalil al-Din Rumi (1207–73), Persia

Change and renewal

93 Speak for me

Watch over me.

Hold your hand before me in protection.

Stand guard for me, speak in defense of me.

As I speak for you, speak for me.

As you speak for me, so I will speak for you.

May all be beautiful before me,

May all be beautiful behind me,

May all be beautiful below me,

May all be beautiful above me,

May all be beautiful all around me.

I am restored in beauty.

Navajo Shootingway ceremony prayer (20th century), USA

94 Earth into gold

O You who change earth into gold,

And out of other earth made the father of humankind,

Change my mistakes and forgetfulness to knowledge.

Jalil al-Din Rumi (1207–73), Persia

95 Music and silence

Silent friend of many distances, feel

How your breath enlarges space. From the dark

Rafters of the belfry let the peal

Of yourself ring out, each bat become a lark,

Singing its exuberance to the harrier.

Be easeful as you morph from shape to shape.

What changed you from a shadow to a warrior?

If the grain tastes bitter, make yourself the grape.

In this tumultuous night flicker as the flame

Of magic at the crossroads where every sense

Meets every other. Live their confluence.

Don't worry if the night forgets your name.

Affirm to the quiet earth: I flow.

Play to the crowded waters, *pianissimo*.

After Rainer Maria Rilke (1875–1926), Sonnets to
Orpheus, *II xxix, Austria*

96 The knife and the apple

I am an apple.

I am not alone

but always have an invisible companion.

Around us his own knife pares the peel and the sweet flesh:

Swish, swish! Swish, swish!

I know that this is nature, willed by the divine.

I rejoice in the companionship of the one who wields the blade.

Modern prayer from San Francisco, USA

97 Serenity prayer

God grant me

Serenity to accept the things I cannot change,

Courage to change the things I can,

And wisdom to know the difference.

Reinhold Niebuhr (1892–1971), USA

98 Meeting rivers

Listen, O Lord of the meeting rivers,

Things standing shall fall

But the moving shall always stay.

St Basavanna (1106–67), India

99 Earth teacher

Earth teach me stillness

As the grasses are stilled with light.

Earth teach me suffering

As old stones suffer with memory.

Earth teach me humility

As blossoms are humble with beginning.

Earth teach me caring

As the mother who secures her young.

Earth teach me courage

As the tree which stands alone.

Earth teach me limitation

As the ant which crawls on the ground.

Earth teach me freedom

As the eagle which soars in the sky.

Earth teach me resignation

As the leaves which die in the autumn.

Earth teach me regeneration

As the seed which rises in the spring.

Earth teach me to forget myself

As melted snow forgets its life.

Earth teach me to remember kindness

As dry fields weep in the rain.

Ute prayer, USA

Old year, new year

100 The gate of the year

And I said to the man who stood at the gate
of the year: "Give me a light that I may tread
safely into the unknown." And he replied: "Go
out into the darkness and put your hand into
the hand of God. That shall be to you better
than a light and safer than a known way."

Minnie Louise Haskins (1875–1957), England

101 Span the world

The world is a bridge.

Pass over it.

Do not build your dwelling there.

*Inscription on the Great Mosque in Fatehpur-Sikri
(17th century), India*

102 Year's end

Year's end, all

corners of this

floating world, swept.

Basho (1644–94), Japan

103 Awareness

Let us not look back in anger or forward in fear,

but around in awareness.

James Thurber (1894–1961), USA

104   The signpost

Life is like a journey.

Each new year is a milestone,

But where is there a signpost,

A guide to the lost life-wanderer?

Hear, from the distant tower

The bells ring down a melodious tune.

From that tower—that giant signpost—

The answer to my question comes down.

Theodor Fontane (1819–98), Germany

105   Resolutions

I will be truthful.

I will suffer no injustice.

I will be free from fear.

I will not use force.

I will be of good will to all men.

Mahatma Gandhi (1869–1948), India

★

Here and now

Health and well-being

106 The power of love

Through love bitter things taste sweet.

Through love pains become as healing balms.

Through love thorns turn into roses.

Through love vinegar becomes sweet wine.

Through love hard stones turn soft like butter.

Through love soft wax becomes hard iron.

Through love grief has the flavor of joy.

Through love stings are like honey.

Through love lions are harmless as mice.

Through love sickness is health.

Through love the dead come to life.

Through love the king is humble as a slave.

Jalil al-Din Rumi (1207–73), Persia

107 Prayer for the sick

We pray for the sick. Grant them health, and raise
them up from their sickness and let them have perfect
health of body and soul, for you are the Savior and
Benefactor, you are Lord and King of all. Amen.

St Serapion (d. after 360CE), Egypt

108   Let the mind run free

Just as a bicycle chain may be too tight, so may

one's carefulness and conscientiousness be so

tense as to hinder the running of one's mind.

William James (1842–1910), USA

109   The clear path

All is transient.

When you perceive this, you are above suffering;

The path is clear.

All is suffering.

When you perceive this, you are above suffering;

The path is clear.

All is unreal.

When you perceive this, you are above suffering;

The path is clear.

The Buddha (c.563–c.483BCE), India

110   In sickness

Lord, you gave me health, and I forgot you.

Now it has been taken away, and I come back to you.

All is yours; you are my Lord.

I offer you everything: my suffering and my healing.

Take all the things that possess me,

so that I may be wholly yours.

After a prayer by François Fénelon (1651–1715), France

111 Waiting for results

My health has been tested:

    I am in a limbo of not knowing.

Let me not hasten to conclusions:

    the condition of my body

    is beyond my understanding,

    as the miracles of nature

    are beyond my understanding.

My life is not suspended:

    it continues as before.

The spirit is undimmed.

We cannot expect perfection.

We can only hope to continue.

The spirit leases a beautiful house

    in the earthquake zone.

Thanks to the Divine for the strength

    to be patient.

Modern prayer from Mexico City, USA

112 Beethoven's prayer

O God give me strength to be victorious
over myself, for nothing may chain me to
this life. O guide my spirit, O raise me
from these dark depths, that my soul,
transported through Your wisdom, may
fearlessly struggle upward in fiery flight.
For You alone understand and can inspire me.

*Ludwig van Beethoven (1770–1827), after he realized
that his deafness was incurable, Germany*

113 The dragon in the cave of flesh

A prayer for help in dealing with pain

I feel that a dragon has been using my body as his den.

His snortings and convulsions are painful to me.

And the pain has taken me to the brink

of hopelessness.

Please help me, Lord, in any of these ways:

May the dragon leave my body, on a whim.

May his visits become shorter.

May I learn that he can be tolerated

if only I can gain the strength to tame him.

May I gain the strength to tame him.

May my rescuers work well and drive the dragon from my

body, with God's blessing.

May I understand at last that there was never any dragon—

it was only one part of my body

sending to another part of my body

urgent messages in my sickness.

Modern prayer from Sicily, Italy

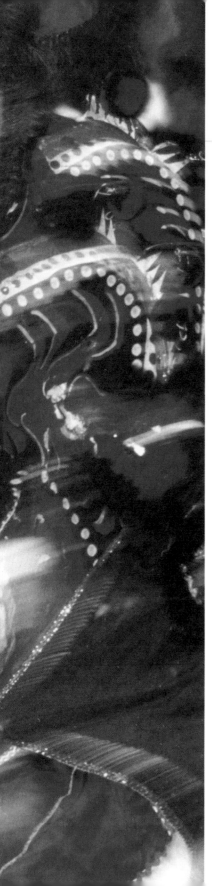

114 For a friend in sickness

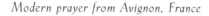

All gifts I might receive from God today

    I offer to the heavens

    with this prayer:

May my friend from his sickbed see

    heartening new horizons roll back

    from his suffering.

Modern prayer from Avignon, France

115 Before an operation

Before my operation I turn to You, because You are always beside me.

You created the healing powers of my body and the strength and courage

of my spirit. They are Your gifts to carry me from fear to confidence.

Modern Jewish prayer

116 A child is ill

Some pray: Let me not lose my little child!

Instead pray: Let me not fear to lose him!

Pray in this spirit, and wait for the outcome.

Marcus Aurelius (121–180), Roman emperor

Friendship

117 Hospitality

I saw a stranger today.

I put food for him in the eating place

and drink in the drinking place

and music in the listening place.

In the Holy Name of the Trinity

he blessed myself and my house,

my goods and my family.

And the lark said in her warble:

Often, often, often

Goes Christ in the stranger's guise

O, often often often

Goes Christ in the stranger's guise.

Traditional Celtic prayer

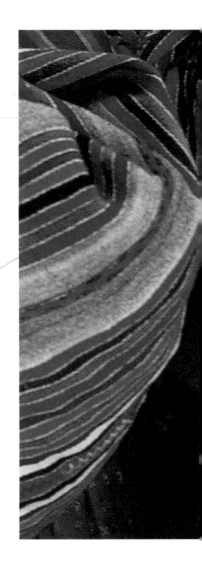

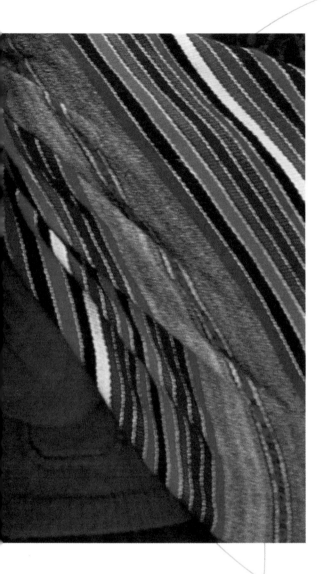

118 New friends

Lord, today you have made us known

to friends we did not know,

and you have given us seats in homes

which are not our own.

You have brought the distant near,

and made a brother of a stranger.

Forgive us Lord ...

we did not introduce you.

Polynesian prayer

119 Love of others

Eternal goodness,

you want me to gaze into you

and see that you love me.

You love me freely,

and you want me to love and serve my neighbors

with the same love,

offering them my prayers and my possessions,

as far as in me lies.

O God, come to my assistance!

St Catherine of Siena (1347–80), Italy

120 Opening the door of bliss

The Friend is the key and I am the lock.

Jalil al-Din Rumi (1207–73), Persia

121 Seeing with new eyes

God our Mother and Father, we come to you

as children. Be with us as we learn to see one

another with new eyes, hear one another with

new hearts, and treat one another in a new way.

Corrymeela Community (20th century), Northern Ireland

122 Making friends

Lord,

show us where there is loneliness,

that we may take friendship.

Show us where individuals are not seen as persons,

that we may acknowledge their identity.

Show us where there is alienation,

that we may take reconciliation.

Prayer for Women's World Day of Prayer, Jamaica

123 A friend's duties

Help me not to abuse my power with friends
and familiars—let me be generous, courteous
and benevolent, let me treat them as I treat
myself, and let me be as good as my word.

After a Buddhist saying

124 The "isness" of others

O Creator Lord, let me feel the "isness" of
things and people, without resistance, without
trying to impose my own pattern upon them or
exploit them for selfish ends. Let me welcome
them, enjoy them, value them, love them, for
what they are and for what they are becoming
through your creative love.

George Appleton (1902–93), England

125 Praying together

To pray together, in whatever tongue or ritual,

is the most tender union of hope and sympathy

that we can contract in this life.

Madame de Staël (1766–1817), France

Family

126 Complete love

At sunrise everything is luminous but not clear.

It is those we live with and love and should know who elude us.

You can love completely without complete understanding.

Norman Maclean (1902–90), from A River Runs Through It, *Canada*

127 The perfect chord

The diversity in the family should be the cause of love and

harmony, as it is in music where many different notes blend

together in the making of a perfect chord.

From the Baha'i scriptures, Persia

128 Finetuning

Far from my family I am traveling on a long journey.

Being so distant,

    I will adjust the sun so that it shines on them more evenly.

    I will adjust the clouds so that they have rain when they need rain,

    blue skies when they need to be happy.

I will adjust the stars so that their destinies turn out

    the way I've always hoped.

My prayers will be my jeweler's screwdriver.

Modern prayer from Singapore

129   Indestructible love

The winter will lose its cold,

as the snow will be without whiteness,

the night without darkness,

the heavens without stars,

the day without light.

The flower will lose its beauty,

all fountains their water,

the sea its fish,

the tree its birds,

the forest its beasts,

the earth its harvest—

all these things will pass before

anyone breaks the bonds of our love,

and before I cease caring for you in

my heart.

May your days be happy in number as

flakes of snow.

May your nights be peaceful,

and may you be without troubles.

Matthew of Rievaulx (13th century), France

130 Ancestors

Oh Great Spirit of our Ancestors,

I raise my pipe to you,

to your messengers the four winds, and to

Mother Earth who provides for your children.

Give us the wisdom to teach our children to

love, to respect and to be kind to each other

so that they may grow with peace in mind.

Let us learn to share all the good things

that you provide for us on this Earth.

Native American prayer

131 Mother's prayer

I turn to you in awe because you have

put your trust in me. I bless you for

the love which binds me to my child;

and for the wonder of creation which

you have renewed within my heart.

Modern prayer, anonymous

132 Telajune, my grandmother

My grandmother would rise and take my arm,

then sifting through the petals in my palm

would place in mine the whitest of them all:

"Salaam, dokhtaré-mahé-man, salaam!"

"Salaam, my daughter lovely-as-the-moon!"

Would that the world could see me, Telajune,

through your eyes! Or that I could see a world

that takes such care to tend what fades so soon.

Mimi Khalvati (b.1944), from "Rubaiyat", England

133 Love and independence

My mother and father still see me as their child—

not fully understanding that I am a child of the spirit.

I will love them always.

I will never challenge their incomplete understanding.

The spirit is theirs as much as mine.

Modern prayer from Harvard University, USA

Stirrings of new life

134 Clouds of glory

Our birth is but a sleep and a forgetting;

The soul that rises with us, our life's star,

Hath had elsewhere its setting,

And cometh from afar:

Not in entire forgetfulness,

And not in utter nakedness,

But trailing clouds of glory do we come

From God, who is our home.

From a poem by William Wordsworth (1770–1850), England

135 Father to mother

My love,

I thank you for the pilgrimage that brought

you to this moment as I deliver our child

back into your arms for the very first time.

Modern affirmation from Sydney, Australia

136 A midwife's blessing

A little drop of the sky,

a little drop of the land,

a little drop of the sea,

on your forehead, beloved one.

To protect, to shield and to surround you.

The little drop of the Three, to fill you

with the graces.

After a traditional Celtic prayer

137 For a newborn

I lift up this newborn child to you.

You brought it to birth, you gave it life.

This child is a fresh bud on an ancient tree,

A new member of an old family.

May this fresh bud blossom.

May this child grow strong and righteous.

Kalahari Bushmen's song, Africa

138 A child's message

Every child comes into the world with the
message that God does not despair of man.

Rabindranath Tagore (1861–1941), India

139 The unborn child

I am not yet born, console me.

I fear that the human race may with tall walls wall me,

with strong drugs dope me, with wise lies lure me,

on black racks rack me, in blood-baths roll me.

I am not yet born; provide me

With water to dandle me, grass to grow for me, trees to talk

to me, sky to sing to me, birds and white light

in the back of my mind to guide me.

Louis MacNeice (1907–63), from "Prayer before birth", Ireland

A child sets out

140 Life's yearning

Your children are not truly your children. They are

the sons and daughters of life's yearning for itself.

Kahlil Gibran (1883–1931), from The Prophet, *Lebanon*

141 A child's question

A child said *What is grass?* fetching it to me with full hands;

How could I answer the child? I do not know what it is any

    more than he.

I guess it must be the flag of my disposition, out of hopeful

    green stuff woven.

Or I guess it is the handkerchief of the Lord,

A scented gift and remembrancer designedly dropt,

Bearing the owner's name someway in the corners, that

    we may see and remark and say, *Whose?*

Walt Whitman (1819–92), from "Song of Myself", USA

142 First steps

After you were born, every minute brought a new miracle:

the flowering of a new life,

the training of a new adventurer.

May your adventures seem miraculous to yourself.

May you one day know it is not to me you must give thanks.

Modern prayer from Edinburgh, Scotland

143   Answers and stories

I pray that my love for you will brim with practical wisdom,

    that where appropriate

    I will be able to respond to your questions with clear answers.

I pray that my love for you will brim with imagination,

    that where appropriate

    I will be able to answer your quesions with enlightening stories.

Modern prayer from Uppsala, Sweden

144   The branching tree

When my child falls in love, let me give thanks.

When my child finds that love can be forever,

    let me give thanks.

This branching tree will always be my home.

From deep in the canopy of leaves I will look down

    upon the birth of my great-great-great-great

    grandchild.

Modern prayer from Wales

145 Experience

I stepped from Plank to Plank

A slow and cautious way

The Stars about my Head I felt

About my Feet the Sea.

I knew not but the next

Would be my final inch—

This gave me that precarious Gait

Some call Experience.

Emily Dickinson (1830–86), USA

146 Heirloom

The world was not left us by our parents,

it was lent us by our children.

African proverb

Between four walls

147 The whole house

God bless the house,

From site to stay,

From beam to wall,

From end to end,

From ridge to basement,

From floor to roof-tree,

From ford to summit,

Ford and summit.

Celtic blessing

148 The home's crossroads

Welcome to our house.

Here is the room

we are most proud of—

the kitchen,

crossroads of friendship

and the world's blessings.

Modern prayer from Bilbao, Spain

149 A still place

Make me

a still place of light

a still place of love

of you

your light radiating

your love vibrating

your touch and your healing

far flung and near

to the myriads caught

in darkness, in sickness

in lostness, in fear

make a heart-center here,

Light of the World.

Prayer from Malling Abbey, Denmark

150 Household spirit

If there must be a god in the house, must be,

Saying things in the rooms and on the stair,

Let him move as the sunlight moves on the floor,

Or moonlight, silently, as Plato's ghost

Or Aristotle's skeleton. Let him hang out

His stars on the wall. He must dwell quietly.

Wallace Stevens (1879–1955), from "Less and Less Human,
O Savage Spirit", USA

151 A home for love

When you stand outside my thatched hut,

Could you guess how spacious it is inside?

There is a galaxy of worlds in here,

And space for as much love as I can find.

Ishikawa Jozan (17th century), from a Zen poem, Japan

152   Sitting by the window

Why should I despair while your presence

between these walls still falls on me, gently,

as moonlight on a seat beside the window.

Rainer Maria Rilke (1875–1926), Austria

153   Climbing the stairs

By gradual steps I rise to the topmost attic of this

house, from which the views are spectacular.

I could rise to the palace of heaven if there were

steps enough.

Let me take two or three steps to the palace of

heaven each day.

Let me think of being a little better, a little kinder,

a little more grateful to you for your gifts, each

time I climb these stairs.

Modern prayer from Jerusalem, Israel

154 The genius of the place

Except the Lord build the house, they labor
in vain that build it.

Psalms *127:1*

155 Prosperity

May your house be full of gifts, crystal and gold,
carnelian and lapis lazuli,
earrings and filigree ornaments, fine new clothes.

From the Epic of Gilgamesh, *Tablet 7 (c.2000BCE), Mesopotamia*

156 Within this house

Within this house, may obedience conquer
disobedience and may peace triumph over discord
here, and generous giving over avarice, reverence
over contempt, speech with truthful words over
lying utterance; may the righteous order gain
victory over the demon of the lie.

From the Yasna *(549–330BCE), a Zoroastrian text, Persia*

157 Gateway to the kingdom

O God, make the door of this house wide enough
to receive all who need human love and friendship,
but narrow enough to shut out all envy, pride
and malice.

Make its threshold smooth enough to be no
stumbling-block to children, nor to straying feet,
but strong enough to turn away the power of evil.

God, make the door of this house a gateway
to your eternal kingdom.

*Thomas Ken (1637–1711), a prayer placed at the door of
a Christian hospital, England*

Plans and projects

158 Prayer for strength

O Lord, I do not pray for tasks equal to my strength:

I ask for strength equal to my tasks.

Philips Brooks (1835–93), USA

159 Facing the truth

From the cowardice that dare not face new truth,

From the laziness that is contented with half-truth,

From the arrogance that thinks it knows all truth,

Good Lord, deliver us.

Modern prayer from Kenya

160 The day's duties

When I awake I feel the stiffness in my limbs.

I will forget my aches and pains

in proportion to my waking up to God

and the memory of what I have to do for him today.

Modern prayer from Baghdad, Iraq

161 Fishing trip

Dear God, be good to me;

The sea is so wide,

And my boat is so small.

Breton fisherman's prayer

162　Be a guiding light

Be generous in prosperity,

and thankful in adversity.

Be fair in judgment,

and guarded in your speech.

Be a lamp to those who walk in darkness,

and a home to the stranger.

Be eyes to the blind,

and a guiding light to the feet of the erring.

Be a breath of life to the body of humankind,

a dew to the soil of the human heart,

and a fruit upon the tree of humility.

Baha'i prayer, Persia

163　Exploring

Help us to be immune from doubts, notions and
illusions which shroud our heart and prevent us
from exploring the hidden mysteries.

Sufi prayer

164 Looking forward

I embark upon this project with a modest prayer:

that its outcome

will be the best that is possible

in whatever circumstances

have unfolded

by the time of its conclusion.

Now let me roll up my shirtsleeves.

Modern prayer from Tokyo, Japan

165 Inevitability

First, there was a mark on paper.

Then many dilemmas and setbacks—even arguments.

The project seemed to be a monster swallowing dreams.

Now the great dome could never not have been.

All great achievements annihilate unlikelihood—

like crusades into the past to remedy errors of omission.

Modern prayer from Rome, Italy

Away from home

166   On a voyage

You, O God, are the Lord of the mountains and the valleys. As I
travel over mountains and through valleys, I am beneath your
feet. You surround me with every kind of creature. Peacocks,
pheasants and wild boars cross my path. Open my eyes to see
their beauty, that I may perceive them as the work of your hands.
In your power, in your thought, all things are abundant.

Sioux prayer, USA

167   The open road

Afoot and light-hearted I take to the open road,

Healthy, free, the world before me,

The long brown path before me leading wherever I choose.

Henceforth I ask not good fortune, I myself am good fortune,

Henceforth I whimper no more, postpone no more, need nothing,

Done with indoor complaints, libraries, querulous criticisms,

Strong and content I travel the open road.

Walt Whitman (1819–92), from "Song of the Open Road", USA

168 Overcoming separation

My God and my Lord:

eyes are at rest, the stars are setting,

hushed are the movements of birds in their nests,

of monsters in the deep.

And you are the Just who knows no change,

the Equity that does not swerve,

the Everlasting that never passes away.

The doors of kings are locked

and guarded by their henchmen.

But your door is open to those who call upon you.

My Lord, each lover is now alone with his beloved.

And I am alone with You.

Rabi'ah al-Adawiyah (c.717–801), India

169 For the journey

The Lord be with you as you go,

Bless you in your coming.

The Presence be with your journey,

Bless the road as it unwinds.

Traditional Celtic prayer

170 Traveler's prayer

Be you a bright flame before me,

Be you a smooth way below me,

Be you a guiding star above me,

Be you a watchful eye behind me,

This day, this night, for ever.

St Columba (c.521–97), Ireland

171 Among dangers

Keep us safe from every ill,

Every mishap, every pain.

Let no men or animals attack us.

Lord, bring us safely home.

Kalahari Bushmen's song, Africa

172   The daring soul

Away O Soul, hoist instantly the anchor!

Cut the hawsers—haul out—shake out every sail!

Sail forth—steer for the deep waters only;

Reckless O Soul, exploring, I with thee, and thou with me,

For we are bound where mariner has not yet dared to go,

And we will risk the ship, ourselves and all.

O my brave Soul.

O farther, farther sail!

O daring joy, but safe! Are they not all the seas of God?

O farther, farther, farther sail!

Walt Whitman (1819–92), from "The Explorers", USA

173 Foundations

O God, you are my rock, my rescue, and

my refuge, I leave it all quietly to you.

George Appleton (1902–93), England

174 Signposts

Speech and custom here are strange to me.

Even the signposts of the heart are in

different tongues, even in different alphabets.

Yet they all point the same way:

I cannot lose myself.

Modern meditation from Hong Kong, China

175 The traveler's cloak

As I travel through the night

Protect me with a cloak of

Heaven's shining might

Moon's floating light

Fire's passionate flare

Ocean's swirling depth

Earth's grounding patience

Wind's soaring wildness

Owl's piercing eyesight

After an Icelandic prayer

176 Mention of God

Blessed is the spot,

and the house,

and the place,

and the city,

and the heart,

and the mountain,

and the refuge,

and the cave,

and the valley,

and the land,

and the sea,

and the island,

and the meadow

where mention of God has been made

and His praise glorified.

Baha' Ullah (1817–92), Persia

Fortune's wheel

177 Heaven's appointments

The superior person is quiet and calm, waiting patiently

for heaven's appointments. The inferior person treads a

dangerous way, always on the look-out for good fortune.

Confucius (551–479BCE), China

178 Change

Everything can change!

May dark Fate rule as it pleases.

Be courageous! On the steepest track,

Trust in luck! Trust in God!

Ascend, despite crashing waves and weathers,

Brave, like Caesar, in his ship.

Friedrich von Matthisson (1761–1831), Germany

179 Gain and loss

Prefer the truth and right by which you seem to lose,

to the falsehood and wrong by which you seem to gain.

Maimonides (1135–1204), Spain

★

180 Fate

Do not call Fate terrible, do not call its end

jealousy; its law is eternal truth, its mercy

godly clarity, its power necessity.

Johann Gottfried von Herder (1744–1803), Germany

181 Tempest-tossed

Lord of the elements and changing seasons, keep

me in the hollow of your hand. When I am tossed

to and fro by the winds of adversity and the blasts

of sickness and misunderstanding, still my racing

heart, quieten my troubled mind.

Brother Ramon (b.1935), from Earth and Seasons, *England*

182 Give and take

Fate does not withdraw anything it
did not give in the first place.

Seneca (c.4BCE–c.65CE), Rome

183 The way to God

On the way to God the difficulties

Feel like being ground by a millstone,
Like night coming at noon, like
Lightning through the clouds.

But don't worry!
What must come, comes.
Face everything with love,
As your mind dissolves in God.

Lal Ded (b.1326), Kashmir

★

184 Happiness made, not found

It is God's will that not only should we be happy,

but that we should create our own happiness—

This is the true moral.

Immanuel Kant (1724–1804), Germany

185 The ground on which I stand

I am of the nature to grow old:

There is no way to escape growing old.

I am of the nature to have ill-health:

There is no way to escape having ill-health.

I am of the nature to die:

There is no way to escape death.

All that is dear to me and everyone I love

are of the nature to change:

There is no way to escape being separated from them.

My actions are my only true belongings:

I cannot escape the consequences of my actions.

My actions are the ground on which I stand.

The Buddha (c.563–c.483BCE), India

186 Strength through adversity

Thought shall be the keener,

heart the harder,

courage the greater,

as our might lessens.

Anglo-Saxon poem (c.1000)

187 The wheel of the heart

Humility rises: the view broadens.

Pride falls: the view narrows.

This is the greater wheel,

alongside the Wheel of Chance.

Modern prayer from London, England

Celebration

188 Laughter

The most wasted of all days is one without laughter.

Sébastien-Roch Nicolas Chamfort (1740/41–94), France

189 This flowery Earth

Let us rejoice while we walk here on this flowery Earth;

May the end never come of our flowers and songs,

But may they continue in the mansion

Of the Giver of Life.

Modern celebration, anonymous

190 Singing praises

Sing praises of the Lord with heart and soul.

Singing, heart, embrace the spirit.

The notes play, like the stars that sparkle,

joyously around the holy name of the Lord.

N.F.S. Grundtvig (1783–1872), Denmark

191 Marriage blessing

May these vows and this marriage be blessed.

May this marriage be delicious milk,

    like wine and halvah.

May it offer fruit and shade,

    like the date palm.

May this marriage be full of laughter,

    making every day a day in Paradise.

May this marriage be a token of compassion,

    a seal of joy now and for ever more.

May this marriage have a gracious face and a good name,

    an omen as welcome

    as the moon in a clear daylight sky.

I have run out of words to describe

    how spirit mingles in this marriage.

Jalil al-Din Rumi (1207–73), Persia

192 Rejoice

Let us rejoice in God's free gift of reason.

Razi (c.864–c.930), Persia

193 Celebrating the snail

Look at this snail's bridlepath, like the Milky Way!

Let us track the snail to its heavenly home.

Let us watch its antlers turn to hear our prayers.

Let us leave our shells behind and rejoice in the

snail's playground.

Modern prayer from South Devon, England

194 Anniversaries

Beautiful paper, silver, gold, ruby, diamond—

worthy things to name our heart's anniversaries.

Modern prayer from Siena, Italy

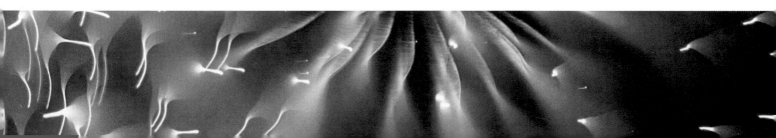

195 The spirit in my heart

This is the spirit that is in my heart, smaller than a grain of rice, or a grain of barley, or a grain of mustard seed, or a grain of canary-seed, or the kernel of a grain of canary-seed; this is the spirit that is in my heart, greater than the Earth, greater than the sky, greater than heaven itself, greater than all these worlds. This is the spirit that is in my heart.

From the Chandogya Upanishad (600–300BCE), a Hindu scripture, India

196 A special day

Because the birthday of my life

Is come, my love is come to me.

Christina Rossetti (1830–94), England

197 Bliss

Now may every living thing, young or old,

weak or strong, living near or far, known or

unknown, living or departed or yet unborn,

may every living thing be full of bliss.

The Buddha (c.563–c.483BCE), India

198 Fellow feelings

My heart is at your festival.

William Wordsworth (1770–1850), England

199 Enjoy the world

You never enjoy the world aright, until the Sea itself flows in your veins, until you are clothed with the heavens, and crowned with the stars: and perceive yourself as the sole heir of the whole world, and more than that, because people are in it who are every one sole heirs as well as you. Until you can sing and rejoice and delight in God, as misers do in gold, and Kings in sceptres, you never enjoy the world ...

Thomas Traherne (1637–74), England

200 A spark from God

Joy, beautiful spark from God,

Daughter of Elysium,

Drunk with fire we enter,

Oh heavenly one, your holy place.

Your magic binds together

What was strictly divided.

All people are made brothers,

Wherever your gentle wing rests.

Friedrich von Schiller (1759–1805), from Ode to Joy, *Germany*

201 Awe

O Lord! Increase my astonishment of You!

Baha'i prayer, Persia

202 Anniversary of love

Dropping a bucket in the well of our beginnings,

we taste again the waters of our contentment.

This well we have built together.

Let us make wishes here.

Let us make wishes for our health and happiness,

and for our children.

One wish we need never make:

that our well never run dry.

Modern prayer from Brittany, France

Times of darkness

203 Lighten our darkness

O Eternal Light, shine into our hearts;

Eternal Goodness, deliver us from despair;

Eternal Power, be you our support;

Eternal wisdom, scatter our ignorance.

After Alcuin (735–804), England

204 Perfect faith

That man is perfect in faith who can come

to God in the utter dearth of his feelings

and desires, without a glow or aspiration,

with the weight of low thoughts, and say

to him: "You are my refuge."

George Macdonald (1824–1905), Scotland

205   Uses of adversity

Our real blessings often appear to us in the

shapes of pains, losses and disappointments;

but let us have patience, and we soon shall

see them in their proper figures.

Joseph Addison (1672–1719), England

206   Looking for answers

Have patience with everything unresolved in your heart

and try to love the questions themselves ...

Don't search for the answers,

they could not be given to you now,

because you would not be able to live them.

And the point is, to live everything.

Live the questions now.

Perhaps then, someday in the future,

you will gradually, without even noticing it,

live your way into the answer.

Rainer Maria Rilke (1875–1926), Austria

207 Writing a letter

Just as day declines to evening, so often after
some little pleasure my heart declines into
depression. Everything seems dull, every action
feels like a burden. If anyone speaks, I scarcely
listen. If anyone knocks, I scarcely hear. My heart
is as hard as flint. Then I go out into the field to
meditate, to read the holy scriptures, and I write
down my deepest thoughts in a letter to you.
And suddenly your grace, dear Jesus, shatters
the darkness with daylight, lifts the burden,
relieves the tension. Soon tears follow sighs, and
heavenly joy floods over me with the tears.

Aelred of Rievaulx (c.1110–67), England

208 Trust in God

May nothing move you;

May nothing terrify you;

Everything passes;

God never changes.

Patience be all to you.

Who trusts in God

Shall never be needy.

God alone suffices.

St Teresa of Avila (1515–82), Spain

209 Songs of beauty

Even from a dark night songs

of beauty may be born.

Modern prayer by
Maryanne Radmacker-Hershey, USA

210 Do not part me from you

O my God do not part me from you.

Do not part me from your sight.

To love you is my faith and belief.

Do not part my belief from my faith.

I've withered, become like autumn.

Do not part the leaves from the branch.

My Master is a rose, I am his leaf.

Do not part the leaf from the rose.

I am a nightingale in my love's garden.

Do not part his beak from his song.

All the fish breathe in water.

Do not part the fish from the lake.

Esrefoglu (d.1469), Turkey

211 Time spent worrying

Where there is pain, cures will be found.

Where there is poverty, wealth will be supplied.

Where there are questions, answers will be given.

Spend less time worrying, and more time trusting.

Jalil al-Din Rumi (1207–73), Persia

212 A shower of mercy

When the heart is hard and parched up, come upon me

    with a shower of mercy.

When grace is lost from life, come with a burst of song.

When tumultuous work raises its din on all sides, shutting me

    out from beyond, come to me, my Lord of silence, with

    thy peace and rest.

When my beggarly heart sits crouched, shut up in a corner, break

    open the door, my king, and come with the ceremony of a king.

When desire blinds the mind with delusion and dust, O thou holy

    One, thou wakeful, come with thy light and thy thunder.

Rabindranath Tagore (1861–1941), India

213 Enlighten my heart

O Lord, enlighten my heart, which

evil desire has darkened—

O Lord, grant me thought of good.

St John Chrysostom (345–407), Turkey

214 Dispel darkness

O merciful Lord, enlighten me with a clear

shining inward light, and remove away all

darkness from the habitation of my heart.

Repress my many wandering thoughts ...

Thomas à Kempis (1379/80–1471), Germany

215 In extremity

Hear my prayer, O Lord;

    let my cry come to you.

Do not hide your face from me

    in the day of my distress.

Psalm *102:1–2*

216 The pathway of peace

From this fog-bound Earth of ours

We take refuge in you.

O rest of our souls,

Escaping like birds from a broken cage

To the keen, clear air, and the sunny uplands

Where you dwell, and with you

Find release from meanness of spirit,

From jealousy, slander, hypocrisy,

From selfish ambition,

From the insidious darkness that broods

And breeds in our wills and hides

The vision of good and the pathway of peace.

We take refuge in you:

Let us walk honestly in the daylight.

John S. Hoyland (1830–94), England

217 Sword and fire

Invisible is the One to mortal eyes,

beyond thought and beyond change.

Know that the One is, and cease from sorrow.

From the Bhagavad Gita *(1st–2nd century), India*

218 Psalm for a stalled heart

My heart is cold today, O God,

    I feel no burning desire,

      no zeal to pray or be with you.

My heart is frozen by the chill of emptiness—

    sluggish and stalled.

Send forth your Spirit

    to revive my heart.

Spark it with a relish for service,

    with a longing to pray.

And may my desire

    to be your flame of warmth and love

    spark other stalled souls

    to come alive, aflame in you.

Modern prayer by Edward Hays, USA

Jouney's end

219 More day to dawn

The light which puts out our eyes is darkness to us.

Only that day dawns to which we are awake. There is

more day to dawn. The sun is but a morning star.

Henry David Thoreau (1817–62), from Walden, USA

220 Anniversary of love

The tall forest towers:

Its cloudy foliage lowers

Ahead, shelf above shelf:

Its silence I hear and obey

That I might lose my way

And myself.

Edward Thomas (1878–1917), from "Lights Out", England

221 Sundown

My task accomplished and the long day done,

My wages taken, and in my heart

Some late lark singing,

Let me be gathered to the quiet West,

The sundown splendid and serene.

William Ernest Henley (1849–1903), England

222 Psalm of battle

God is praise and glory;

Therefore glory and praise be unto Him

Who led me by the hand in stony places,

Who gave me a treasure of gold and a throne of gold

And set a sword of victory in my hand!

We died, we died in the battle,

But He has set us upon happy grass

Beside an eternal river of scented honey.

From 1001 Nights (13th century), Arabia

223 Light the way

From one darkness

Into another darkness

I soon must go.

Light the long way before me,

Moon on the mountain rim!

Lady Izumi Shikibu (c.970–1030), Japan

224 I so liked spring

I so liked spring last year

   because you were here;—

     The thrushes too—

Because it was these you so liked to hear—

    I so liked you.

   This year's a different thing,—

    I'll not think of you.

But I'll like spring because it is simply spring

    As the thrushes do.

Charlotte Mew (1869–1928), England

225 One equal light

Bring us, O Lord, at our last awakening

into the house and gate of heaven,

to enter into that gate and dwell in that house

where there shall be no darkness nor dazzling,

   but one equal light;

no noise nor silence, but one equal music;

no fears nor hopes, but one equal possession;

no ends nor beginnings, but one equal eternity

in the habitations of your glory and dominion,

world without end.

John Donne (1572–1631), England

226 Bereavement

When I am dead, cry for me a little,

Think of me sometimes, but not too much.

Think of me now and again, as I was in life.

At some moments it's pleasant to recall, but not for long.

Leave me in peace, and I shall leave you in peace.

And while you live, let your thoughts be with the living.

Traditional Native American prayer, USA

227 In the next room

Death is nothing at all:

I have only slipped away into the next room.

I am I and you are you;

Whatever we were to each other, that we are still.

Call me by my old familiar name,

Speak to me in the easy way which you always used.

Put no difference in your tone;

Wear no forced air or solemnity or sorrow.

Laugh as we always laughed at the little jokes we enjoyed together.

Play, smile, think of me, pray for me.

Why should I be out of mind because I am out of sight?

I am but waiting for you, for an interval, somewhere very near,

just around the corner.

All is well.

Canon Henry Scott Holland (1847–1918), England

228 The day of death

The day of death is when two worlds meet with a kiss:

this world going out, the future world coming in.

Jewish prayer by Jose ben Abin

229 No fear to die

Teach me your mood, O patient stars,

Who climb each night the ancient sky,

Leaving on space no shade, no scars,

No trace of age, no fear to die.

Ralph Waldo Emerson (1803–82), USA

230 Paradise of delight

O God, give him rest with the devout and the just,

In the place of the pasture of rest

And of refreshment, of waters in the paradise

Of delight, from where grief and pain and sighing

Have fled away.

Holy, holy, holy O God,

Heaven and Earth are full of your holy glory.

Egyptian commendation (5th century)

In touch with spirit

The power of prayer

231 Rising from prayer

Who rises from prayer a better man,

his prayer is answered.

George Meredith (1828–1909), England

232 Before prayer

I weave a silence on my lips

I weave a silence into my mind

I weave a silence within my heart

I close my ears to distractions

I close my eyes to attractions

I close my heart to temptations.

Modern prayer by David Adam, from
Edge of Glory, *England*

233 Closeness

Him to whom you pray is closer to

you than the neck of your camel.

Muhammad (c.570–632), Arabia

234 The world in tune

Prayer is

The world in tune,

A spirit-voice,

And vocal joys

Whose *echo* is heaven's bliss.

Henry Vaughan (1622–95), Wales

Living in the spirit

235 Growing circles

I live my life in growing circles

that stretch across all things.

I may not complete the last circle

but I will attempt it.

I circle about God, about the age-old tower,

and circle for thousands of years.

And I don't yet know: am I a falcon, a storm

or a thundering song?

Rainer Maria Rilke (1875–1926), Austria

236 A heart of flame

To my God a heart of flame,

To my fellow men a heart of love,

To myself a heart of steel.

St Augustine of Hippo (354–430), North Africa

237 The paradox

Whoever desires to be given everything

must first give everything away.

Meister Eckhart (1260–1327), Germany

238 Let us live joyfully

Let us live joyfully.

Let us form a community of love, in a world full of hatred.

Let us live without any kind of hatred.

Let us live joyfully.

Let us form a community of spiritual health, in a world full of illness.

Let us live without any kind of spiritual disease.

Let us live joyfully.

Let us form a community of peace, in a world full of rivalry.

Let us live without any kind of rivalry.

Let us live joyfully.

Let us form a community which possesses nothing.

Let us live on spiritual bliss, radiating spiritual light.

From the Dhammapada, part of the Pali canon (c.500BCE–c.200CE), India

239　The inward soul

Give me beauty in the inward soul; and may the outward

and inward person be at one.

May I reckon the wise to be the wealthy, and may I have

such a quantity of gold as a

temperate man can bear and carry—

Anything more? This prayer, I think, is enough for me.

Socrates (469–399BCE), Athens

240 Profit from love

The days are of most profit

to him who acts in love.

Traditional Jainist saying

241 The good life

The good life is one inspired by

love and guided by knowledge.

Bertrand Russell (1872–1970), England

242 Humility

I will conceal the good that I have done

to others, while advertising the good that

others have done to me.

'Ali (c.600–661), first Imam of the Shi'a branch of Islam

243 Simplicity

Pray God, keep us simple.

William Thackeray (1811–63), England

244 Grave goods

After death we remain, our actions

placed beside us in heaps.

From an ancient Egyptian text (c.2100BCE)

245 After rain

A single gentle rain makes the grass many shades greener. So our prospects brighten on the influx of better thoughts.

Henry David Thoreau (1817–62), from Walden, USA

246 Disarm evil thoughts

Just as we can't stop birds from flying over our heads, but can stop them from nesting in our hair, so we can't avoid evil thoughts, but we can stop them from taking root in our heart and giving birth to evil deeds.

Martin Luther (1483–1546), Germany

Inspiration and creativity

247 The role of a bard

The Three Foundations of Bardic Knowledge:

The knowledge of song;

The knowledge of bardic secrets;

The wisdom within.

The Three Pleasures of the Bards of Britain:

To speak knowledgeably;

To act wisely;

To bring peace and harmony.

From an ancient Welsh text

248 Seeing and knowing

Unto this darkness which is beyond Light we pray
that we may come, and through loss of sight and
knowledge may see and know that which transcends
sight and knowledge, by the very fact of not seeing
and knowing—for this is real sight and knowledge.

Dionysius (c.500CE), Syria

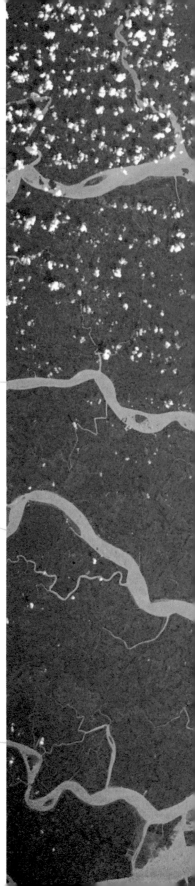

249   Forge new paths

Do not go where the path may lead,

Go instead where there is no path

and leave a trail.

Ralph Waldo Emerson (1803–82), USA

250   Deep within

Dive deep within:

You are bound to hear

The whispering

Peace-sea-messages.

Modern prayer by Sri Chinmoy, USA

251   God in every breath

Dear God, be all my love, all my hope and all my endeavor;

let my thoughts and words emanate from you, let my daily

life be lived in you, and let every breath I take be filled

with joy for you. Amen

After St John Cassian (c.360–435), Scythia

252   Fiery words

Strengthen my tongue that it may

Convey even one single spark of all

Your glory to future generations.

Dante Alighieri (1265–1321), from The Divine Comedy, *Italy*

Everywhere the divine

253 Meditation

I, the blazing life of divine wisdom,

I set alight the beauty of the plains,

I radiate the waters,

I glow in the Sun, and the Moon and the stars.

With wisdom I order all things right.

I beautify the Earth.

I am the breeze that nurtures all things green.

I am the rain coming from the dew

that makes the fields laugh with the pleasure of life.

I call up tears, the perfume of holy work.

I am the yearning for good.

St Hildegard von Bingen (1098–1179), Germany

254 Wisdom and spirit

Wisdom and Spirit of the universe!

You that are the Eternity of Thought!

That gives to forms and images a breath

And everlasting motion!

William Wordsworth (1770–1850), from The Prelude, *England*

255 The source of all answers

I am the wind which blows over the sea,

I am the wave of the ocean, I am the murmur of the billows,

I am the tear of the sun, I am the fairest of plants,

I am a wild boar in valor; I am a salmon in the water.

I am a lake in the plain ...

I am a word of Science; I am the spearpoint which gives victory;

I am the God who creates the fire of thought in humankind.

Who will enlighten each question if not I?

Druid Amergin (c.600BCE), Ireland

256 Eternity

I saw Eternity the other night

Like a great *Ring* of pure endless light,

All calm, as it was bright,

And round beneath it,

Time in hours, days, years

Driven by the spheres

Like a vast shadow moved, in which the world

And all her train were hurled.

Henry Vaughan (1622–95), from "The World", Wales

Thanksgivings

257   The ninefold chorus

We bathe your palms

In the showers of wine,

In the crook of the kindling,

In the seven elements,

In the sap of the tree,

In the milk of honey.

We place nine pure, choice gifts

In your clear beloved face:

The gift of form,

The gift of voice,

The gift of fortune,

The gift of goodness,

The gift of eminence,

The gift of charity,

The gift of integrity,

The gift of true nobility,

The gift of apt speech.

Traditional Gaelic invocation

258   The most amazing day

i thank You God for most this amazing

day:for the leaping greenly spirits of trees

and a blue true dream of sky;and for everything

which is natural which is infinite which is yes

(i who have died am alive again today,

and this is the sun's birthday;this is the birth

day of life and of love and wings:and of the gay

great happening illimitably earth)

how should tasting touching hearing seeing

breathing any — lifted from the no

of all nothing — human merely being

doubt unimaginable You?

(now the ears of my ears awake and

now the eyes of my eyes are opened)

E.E. Cummings (1894–1962), USA

259 Rejoice

Rejoice always, pray without ceasing,

give thanks in all circumstances;

for this is the will of God in

Christ Jesus for you. Do not quench

the Spirit.

1 Thessalonians 5:16–19

260 For the moon

When I give thanks for the moon,

let the moon be a symbol of everything else

for which I feel gratitude.

As I lift my binoculars

to observe its astonishing seas and craters,

I am raising my arms in a prayer of thanksgiving

for the cosmic miracle.

Modern prayer from Alice Springs, Australia

261 My garden

My thoughts are as a garden plot, that knows

No rain but of your giving, and no rose

Except your name. I dedicate it yours,

My garden, full of fruits in harvest time.

Mutamid, king of Seville (1040–95), Spain

262 For gleaming light

O perfect master, you shine on all things and

all people, as gleaming moonlight plays upon

a thousand waters at once!

From the Amidista, a Buddhist spiritual treatise, India

263 For unknown gifts

Thank you for what we might one day

be lucky enough to see, hear, smell,

taste and touch for the first time.

Modern thanksgiving from Warsaw, Poland

264 To the Great Spirit

We return thanks to our mother,

the Earth, which sustains us.

We return thanks to the rivers and streams

which supply us with water.

We return thanks to all herbs, which furnish medicines

for the cure of our diseases.

We return thanks to the corn, and to her sisters,

the beans and squashes, which give us life.

We return thanks to the bushes and trees,

which provide us with fruit.

We return thanks to the wind,

which, moving the air, has banished diseases.

We return thanks to the Moon and the stars,

which have given us their light when the Sun was gone.

We return thanks to our grandfather He-no,

who has protected us from witches and reptiles.

We return thanks to the Sun,

that he has looked upon the Earth with a beneficent eye.

We return thanks to the Great Spirit,

in whom is embodied all goodness,

and who directs all things for the good of his children.

After an Iroquois song (19th century), USA

265 The secret of time

Giving thanks for the moment is the

only way to glimpse eternity.

Modern meditation from Seville, Spain

266 A peaceful foundation

Like weary waves,

thought flows upon thought,

but the still depth beneath

is all thine own.

George Macdonald (1824–1905), Scotland

267 Pied beauty

Glory be to God for dappled things—

    For skies of couple-colour as a brinded cow;

        For rose-moles all in stipple upon trout that swim;

Fresh-firecoal chestnut-falls; finches' wings;

    Landscape plotted and pieced—fold, fallow, and plough;

        And all trades, their gear and tackle and trim.

All things counter, original, spare, strange;

    Whatever is fickle, freckled (who knows how?)

        With swift, slow; sweet, sour; adazzle, dim;

He fathers-forth whose beauty is past change:

                Praise him.

Gerard Manley Hopkins (1844–89), England

268 Moments of fulfillment

We thank you, God, for the moments of fulfillment:

    the end of a day's work,

    the harvest of sugar cane,

    the birth of a child,

for in these pauses, we feel the rhythm of the eternal.

Modern prayer from Hawaii, USA

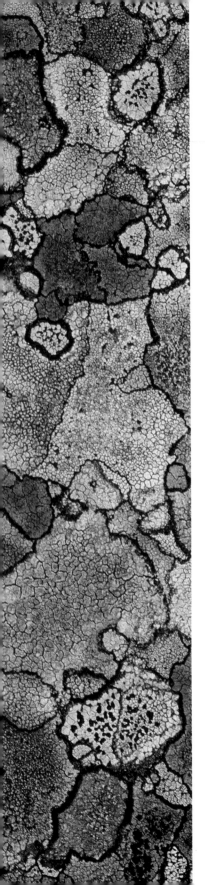

269 For my eyes

Thank you, Lord, for my eyes

    Windows open on the wide world ...

May my look never be one of disappointment,

Disillusionment, despair;

But may it know how to admire, contemplate,

    adore.

Michel Quoist (b.1921), France

270 For music

The music flows within me like pure spirit.

What a wonderful conversation within the flow of universal energy!

Eloquence needs no words—

I know this from my intimacy with the divine.

O Great One, I give thanks for this and for all music—

a power line fed into my heart from the universal grid.

Modern prayer from Vienna, Austria

271 Praise for the Lord of the Earth

We praise the Creator, the Lord of Light.

We praise the Teacher, the Lord of Purity.

We praise the stars, the Moon, the Sun and the trees.

We praise the mountains, the waters, the pastures

    and our homes set among them.

We praise all good men; we praise all good women.

We praise you, our home, O Earth.

We praise you, O God, Lord of the Earth.

After the Zend-Avesta (6th century BCE), a Zoroastrian text, Persia

272 God's gifts

Thanks be to you for the gifts you give me:

Each day, each night, on sea and land,

Each weather, fair, calm or wild,

For your eye watching over me,

For each hour, its ebb, its flow,

For your arm comforting around me:

For each gift thanks be to you.

The best gift is yourself to me.

Adapted from a traditinal Celtic prayer

Forgiveness

273 The abolition of resentment

I have forgotten where the hatchet is buried.

Modern meditation from New Mexico, USA

274 One pure heart

The prayer of one pure heart, I think, has the power

to atone for many.

Sophocles (c.496–406BCE), Athens

275 Transgressions

All that we ought to have thought and have not thought;

All that we ought to have spoken and have not spoken;

All that we ought to have done and have not done;

All that we ought not to have thought and yet have thought;

All that we ought not to have spoken and yet have spoken;

All that we ought not to have done and yet have done;

For thoughts, words and works, pray we, O God, for forgiveness,

And repent with penance.

From the Zend-Avesta (6th century BCE), a Zoroastrian text, Persia

276 O Lord, forgive

Our insensitivity to the needs of others,

> O Lord, forgive.

Our prejudice and fear that prevent us from loving,

> O Lord, forgive.

The narrowness of our vision and our shrinking from your

> demands,

> O Lord, forgive.

Our resentment against those who have hurt us,

> O Lord, forgive.

Our desire to do your work in our way,

> O Lord, forgive.

Our impatiance with those who are different from us,

> O Lord, forgive.

Our failure to listen properly to other points of view,

> O Lord, forgive.

Our fear of coming out of the fortress of our own souls into

> fuller life and deeper love,

> O Lord, forgive.

Modern prayer from Toronto, Canada

277 The magician

We admire the magician who makes doves disappear.

In defiance of what some people call common sense,

    and what other people call being true to one's feelings,

    I make my grievances disappear.

I do not admire myself for this,

    nor expect anyone else to admire me.

Modern affirmation from Helsinki, Finland

278 Prayer for guidance

Forgive, O Lord, what we have been,

Direct what we are,

And order what we shall be,

For your mercy's sake.

Modern prayer, anonymous

279 Love in forgiveness

I forgive you for what you have said and done.

I forgive you for what you believe to be true.

I forgive you for making light of the hurt you have caused.

I forgive you for not saying sorry.

I do not withhold my love.

If I ever do so, please forgive me.

Modern prayer from Tel Aviv, Israel

280 The inner temple

First I enter my inner temple, sprinkle waters

    from the sacred basin in a pure act

    of forgiveness.

Next, to complete my forgiveness, I open wide

    the doors of my inner temple

    to the one I have forgiven.

Modern prayer from Kuala Lumpur, Malaysia

Contemplation of the divine

281 Like a tiger

You are like a tiger, compelling in your beauty,

Yet terrifying in your strength.

You are like a honey-comb on the branch of a tree;

I can see the sweet honey, but the branch is too high for me to climb.

You are like a goldfish swimming in a pond,

Only an arm's length from the bank; yet if I try to catch you in my hand,

You slip from my grasp.

You are like a snake,

Your skin dazzling in its bright colors,

Yet your tongue able to destroy a person with a single prick.

Be merciful to me, O Lord. Give me life, not death.

Reach out to me, and hold me in your arms.

Come down to me, and lift me up to heaven.

Sustain my feeble soul with your power.

Manikka Vasahar (8th century), India

282 Humility

I am a handful of herbs from the garden of your beauty.

I am a thread hanging from the robe of your greatness.

Jalil al-Din Rumi (1207–73), Persia

★

283 The inner self

He is the inner self of all,

Hidden like a little flame in the heart.

Only by the stilled mind can he be known.

Those who realize him become immortal.

From the Upanishads *(600–300BCE), India*

★

284 God's attention

We can with certainty say these things

   about God:

He knows;

He wills;

He speaks;

And he hears.

ibn Sina (980–1037), Arabia

★

285 A love song

Majestic Sovereign, timeless wisdom,

Your kindness melts my hard, cold, soul.

Handsome lover, selfless giver,

Your beauty fills my dull, sad eyes.

I am yours, you made me.

I am yours, you called me.

I am yours, you saved me.

I am yours, you loved me.

I will never leave your presence.

Give me death, give me life.

Give me sickness, give me health.

Give me honor, give me shame.

Give me weakness, give me strength.

I will have whatever you give.

St Teresa of Avila (1515–82), Spain

286 Always present

The ultimate Consciousness

is always present everywhere.

It is beyond space and time,

with no before or after.

It is undeniable and obvious.

So what can be said about it?

Abhinava Gupta (10th century), India

287 Infinity

All around I behold your Infinity: the power of your

innumerable arms, the vision of your innumerable

eyes, the words from your innumerable mouths,

and the fire of life of your innumerable bodies.

Nowhere do I see a beginning or middle or end

of you, O God of all, O Great Infinity.

From the Bhagavad Gita *(1st–2nd century), India*

The path of the divine

288 A potter's wheel

As a potter shapes clay into a vessel,

shape me, O Blessed One,

into a true disciple of your Way.

Fill me with your grace

that I may train my body this day

to serve others.

Modern prayer by Edward Hays, USA

289 Everlasting light

The sun shall no longer be your light by day,

nor for brightness shall the moon give light to

you by night;

but the Lord will be your everlasting light,

and your God will be your glory.

Isaiah *60:19*

290 The divine likeness

Two things I recognize in myself, Lord:

I am made in your image;

I have defaced that likeness.

I admit to my fault.

Take from me what I have spoiled;

Leave in me what you have made.

Brother Kenneth, Community of the
Glorious Ascension, England

291 Bitter-sweet

Ah my dear angry Lord,

Since you do love, yet strike;

Cast down, yet help afford;

Sure I will do the like.

I will complain, yet praise;

I will bewail, approve:

And all my sour-sweet days

I will lament and love.

George Herbert (1593–1633), England

292   The helmsman

Steer the ship of my life, good Lord, to your
quiet harbor, where I can be safe from the
storms of sin and conflict. Show me the
course I should take. Renew in me the gift of
discernment, so that I can always see the
right direction in which I should go. And give
me the strength and the courage to choose
the right course, even when the sea is rough
and the waves are high, knowing that through
enduring hardship and danger in your name
I shall find comfort and peace.

St Basil the Great, Bishop of Caesarea (329–379),
Cappadocia

293 Hymn of Jesus

I am a lamp to you that behold me.

I am a mirror to you that perceive me.

I am a door to you that knock me.

I am a way to you the traveler.

From the apocryphal Acts of John

294 Offer up your soul

Prayer must mean putting one's very soul

    upon our hands,

Offering it to God.

From the Babylonian Talmud (6th century), Persia

295 Purity of mind

When my eyes see some uncleanness,

let not my mind see things that are not clean.

When my ears hear some uncleanness,

let not my mind hear things that are not clean.

Traditional Shinto prayer, Japan

296 An instrument of peace

Lord, make me an instrument of your peace.

Where there is hatred, let me sow love;

Where there is injury, pardon;

Where there is doubt, faith;

Where there is despair, hope;

Where there is darkness, light;

Where there is sadness, joy.

St Francis of Assisi (1181–1226), Italy

297 Shanti

Oh God, lead us from the unreal to the real.

Oh God, lead us from darkness to light.

Oh God, lead us from death to immortality.

Shanti, Shanti, Shanti unto all.

Traditional Hindu prayer
(shanti: peace beyond understanding)

298 Show the way

Go out in a spirit of compassion,

And take to the others the benefits that you have received.

Teach the Way, which is glorious from the beginning to the end.

Urge people to live lives of perfect holiness.

There are many people whose souls would shine brightly but for

    a few specks of dust.

If the Way is not preached to them, they cannot be saved;

But if they hear about the Way, they will follow the Way.

From the Mahavagga, part of the Pali canon (c.500BCE–c.200CE), India

299 On solid ground

May the ground be solid on which I walk.

May my faith soften my tread.

Adapted from a New England hymn

The path of the true self

300 A radiant awakening

Father in heaven, when the thought of you

  wakes in our hearts,

Let it not wake like a frightened bird that

Flies about in dismay, but like a child waking

From its sleep with a heavenly smile.

Søren Kirkegaard (1813–55), Denmark

301 Dance of life

Let your life lightly dance on the edges

of time like a dew on the tip of a leaf.

Rabindranath Tagore (1861–1941), India

302 Shedding light

I am you, O God. You are my being.

You are the fulfillment of my desires.

I embrace you in my innermost thoughts.

Your soul and my soul are like two lamps,

Shedding a single light.

Hallaj (858–922), Iran

303　Samurai warrior's creed

I have no parents—I make the heavens and earth my parents.

I have no home—I make awareness my home.

I have no life or death—I make the tides of breathing my life and death.

I have no divine power—I make honesty my divine power.

I have no means—I make understanding my means.

I have no magic secrets—I make character my magic secret.

I have no body—I make endurance my body.

I have no strategy—I make "unshadowed by thought" my strategy.

I have no miracles—I make right action my miracles.

I have no principles—I make adaptability to all circumstances my principles.

I have no tactics—I make emptiness and fullness my tactics.

I have no talents—I make ready wit my talent.

I have no friends—I make my mind my friend.

I have no enemy—I make carelessness my enemy.

I have no armor—I make benevolence and righteousness my armor.

I have no castle—I make immovable mind my castle.

I have no sword—I make absence of self my sword.

From the Bushido, the code of conduct for the warrior (14th century), Japan

304 Giver of life

O God, You are the Giver of life, the Remover

of pains and sorrows, the Bestower of happiness.

O Creator of the Universe, may we receive

Your supreme sin-destroying light.

May You guide our intellect in the right direction.

From the Rig Veda *(c.1500–c.1000BCE), India*

305 Silent meditation

The sign from God in contemplation is silence,

because it is impossible for anyone to do two things

at once—we cannot both speak and meditate.

Through the faculty of meditation we attain to

eternal life; through it we receive the breath of the

Holy Spirit—the bestowal of the Spirit is given in

reflection and meditation.

Abdu'l-baha (1884–1921), India

306 The pearl

Pearls do not lie on the seashore,

If you desire one you must dive for it.

Oriental proverb

307 Where the mind is without fear

Where the mind is without fear and the head is held high;

Where knowledge is free;

Where the world has not been broken up into fragments by

Narrow domestic walls;

Where words come out from the depth of truth;

Where tireless striving stretches its arms towards perfection;

Where the clear stream of reason has not lost its way into

The dreary desert sand of dead habit;

Where the mind is led forward by thee into ever-widening

Thought and action—

Into that heaven of freedom, my Father, let my country awake.

Rabindranath Tagore (1861–1941), India

308 The music of One

A musician speaks to me eloquently in a language I have never mastered.

For a moment my heart stands still, enlightened.

I understand the music even though the music does not engage my reason.

The One speaks to me eloquently in a language I was never taught.

For the rest of my life my heart stands still, enlightened.

I understand the One even though the One does not engage

   my weaknesses or my fears.

Modern prayer from Amsterdam, Holland

309 Final conquest

O God, help me to victory over myself, for

it is difficult to conquer oneself—though

when that is conquered, all is conquered.

Prayer from a Jain scripture (c.500BCE), India

310 The ten perfections

I shall seek to develop the perfections of generosity,

virtue, doing without, wisdom, energy, forbearance,

truthfulness, resolution, love, serenity.

From the Pali canon (c.500BCE–c.200CE), India

311 The search for rest

You made me for yourself,

And my heart is restless

Until it finds its rest in you.

St Augustine of Hippo (354–430), North Africa

312 One with God

O God—

In your purity you make me pure.

In your wholeness you make me whole.

In my service you serve me.

I bow to all, because I bow to you.

Hallaj (858–922), Iran

313 The river of time

To become enlightened you must cross

the river of time.

All material things pass away,

But enlightenment lasts for all eternity.

*From the Dhammapada, part of the Pali canon
(c.500BCE–c.200CE), India*

314 Looking for God

I am searching for the divine scent

in the world's larder.

I know that one day I will savor it.

Modern prayer from Casablanca, Morocco

315 The voice in my silence

I believe that God is in me as the sun is in
the color and fragrance of a flower—the
Light in my darkness, the Voice in my silence.

Helen Keller (1880–1968), USA

316 The solemn hour

Who now weeps somewhere in the world,

Weeps without cause in the world,

Weeps over me.

Who now laughs somewhere in the night,

Laughs without cause in the night,

Laughs at me.

Who now wanders somewhere in the world,

Wanders without reason in the world,

Wanders to me.

Who now dies somewhere in the world,

Dies without reason in the world,

Looks at me.

Rainer Maria Rilke (1875–1926), Austria

317 Surrender

Take, Lord, all my liberty. Receive my memory, my
understanding and my whole will. Whatever I have and
possess you have given to me; to you I restore it wholly,
and to your will I utterly surrender it for your direction.
Give me the love of you only, with your grace, and I am
rich enough; nor do I ask for anything else.

St Ignatius Loyola (1491–1556), Spain

318 The divine country

Regard Heaven as your father, Earth as your mother,
all things as brothers and sisters, and you will enjoy
the divine country that excels all others.

Traditional Shinto saying (6th century), Japan

319 The mudfish

Live like a mudfish, whose stain is bright and
silvery even though it dwells in mud.

Ramakrishna (1836–86), India

320 Abundant treasure

O Lord, help me. Strengthen my faith and trust in you. In you I have sealed all the treasures I have. I am poor; you are rich and came to be merciful to the poor. I am a sinner; you are upright. With me there is an abundance of sin; in you is the fullness of righteousness. Therefore, I will remain with you from whom I can receive, but to whom I may not give.

Martin Luther (1483–1546), Germany

321 A life of learning

I know that I will never stop learning.

Because I am driven by my love,

which touches the vital lives of others,

much of what I learn will give me joy.

I pray to receive from others the sparks of their inner light,

ignited by the light I cast upon them.

Modern prayer from Ontario, Canada

322 Everlasting beauty

O God! if I worship You in fear of Hell, burn me in Hell; and if I worship You in hope of Paradise, exclude me from Paradise; but if I worship You for Your own sake, withhold not Your Everlasting Beauty!

Rabi'ah al-Adawiyah (c.717–801), India

323 Spiritual union

Help me, O Lord, to descend into the depths of my being, below my conscious and sub-conscious life until I discover my real self, that which is given me from you, the divine likeness in which I am made and into which I am to grow, the place where your Spirit communes with mine, the spring from which all my life rises.

George Appleton (1902–93), England

★

The world at large

Peace

324 Incantation

May there be peace in the higher regions; may there be
peace in the firmament; may there be peace on Earth. May
the waters flow peacefully; may the herbs and plants grow
peacefully; may all the divine powers bring unto us peace.
The supreme Lord is peace. May we all be in peace, peace,
and only peace; and may that peace come into each of us.
Shanti, shanti, shanti!

From the Vedas *(c.1500–c.1000BCE), India*
(shanti: peace beyond understanding)

325 The abyss of peace

O God, you are the unsearchable abyss of peace,

the ineffable sea of love,

and the fountain of blessings.

Water us with plentiful streams

from the riches of your grace;

and from the most sweet springs of your kindness,

make us children of quietness and heirs of peace.

St Clement of Alexandria (c.150–c.215), Egypt

326 Auditioning the choir of peace

Auditioning for the hymn of peace,

all the strangers who were killed or wounded in the war

are accepted unanimously.

Modern meditation from Warsaw, Poland

327 Amity to all

I give amity to all, and enmity to none.

Know that violence is the root-cause of all

    miseries in the world.

Violence, in fact, is the knot of bondage.

"Do not injure any living being."

This is the eternal, perennial, and unalterable

    way of spiritual life.

A weapon, however powerful it may be,

    can always be superseded by a superior weapon;

    however no weapon can

    be superior to non-violence and love.

Jain prayer, India

328   The parachute

From the hearts of peaceful souls

    may a flag of peace unfurl,

    to fall from the sky

    like a vast parachute

    onto a region of war.

May enmities flounder,

    tiring themselves

    to exhaustion beneath the parachute of peace.

Modern prayer from Sarajevo, Bosnia

329   A prayer

In our country they are desecrating churches.

May the rain that pours in pour into the font.

Because no snowflake ever falls in the wrong place,

may snow lie on the altar like an altar cloth.

Michael Longley (b.1939), Northern Ireland

330 Once more

Once more may the houses become homes,

  not monuments of a way of life abandoned.

Once more may the hospital become preoccupied

  by accidents, tumors, and viruses.

Once more may the museum, now a barracks,

  become a museum,

  with an annex on the subject of war,

  in honor of a new and permanent peace.

Modern prayer from Croatia

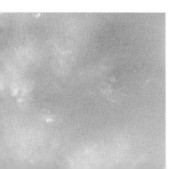

331 The divided city

In this city where gunshots are almost as common as handshakes,

let us pray that two enemies will shake hands.

That makes four hands at peace with each other.

In this city where woundings outnumber healings,

let us pray that the numbers do somersaults.

Modern prayer from Sarajevo, Bosnia

332 The most peaceful place

Men seek out retreats for themselves, cottages in the country, lonely
seashores and mountains. You too are disposed to hanker greatly after
such things: and yet all this is the very commonest stupidity; for it is in
your power, whenever you wish, to retire into yourself: and nowhere is
there any place that a man may retire to that is quieter and more free
from politics than his own soul.

Marcus Aurelius (121–180), Roman emperor

333 Bodies and memories

When I pray for peace

    I do not think of doves, of a symbolic handshake,

    of a football game played in no-man's land

    between the front lines of two opposing armies.

I think of wounds, of a man and woman disabled

    for the rest of their lives.

Let us have peace, so that when they fall in love

    and marry, their bodies and their memories

    have the chance to be whole.

Modern prayer from Brussels, Belgium

334 Aftermath

Imagine among these meadows

Where the soldiers sink to dust

An aftermath with swallows

Lifting blood on their breasts

Up to the homely gables, and like

A dark cross overhead the hawk.

*Michael Longley (b.1939),
Northern Ireland*

335 Meditation

Without meditation, where is peace?

Without peace, where is happiness?

Traditional Hindu saying

Freedom

336 A gleam of silver

The spirit flashes, like a salmon leaping.

Although a salmon may be caught on a hook,

    the fisherman has no way to capture its beauty.

Modern prayer from Inverness, Scotland

★

337 Escape from the wordless prison

For all those whose tongues are in manacles,

    whose pens are suffering from a drought of ink,

    let us pray.

No virtuous thought may be imprisoned for ever.

    As a dove flies out through prison bars,

    our beautiful words, roosting in their cage,

    will soon fly out and flock around the heads of tyrants,

    masking their sun.

Modern prayer from Beijing, China

★

338 Light against dark

Freedom is the pressure of the world's light

against the prison door of our darkness.

Modern meditation from Indonesia

339 The caged robin

A robin redbreast in a cage

Puts all heaven in a rage.

William Blake (1757–1827), England

340 Another world

Our freedom is but a light that breaks

through from another world.

Nikolai Gumilev (1886–1921), Russia

341 Loosen the bonds of suffering

May all beings everywhere plagued with

sufferings of body and mind quickly be freed

from their illnesses. May those frightened

cease to be afraid, and may those bound be

free. May the powerless find power, and may

people think of befriending one another.

Traditional Buddhist prayer

★

★

342 Liberty and growth

Growth is not possible without liberty.

Let us pray for liberty in repressive regimes

so that the people may grow into their birthright.

Modern prayer from New York, USA

Equality

343 On God's side

I outnumber my opponents

One, on God's side, is a majority.

Wendell Phillips (1811–84), USA

344 Justice

O God, to those who have hunger give
   bread,
And to us who have bread give the hunger
   for justice.

Modern prayer from Latin America

345   Sound and light

I rejoice in the sound of democracy:
of my opponents voicing their best arguments.

I rejoice in the possibility that the light
by which I live may be criticized by others
for being sited on a wrong headland.

Modern prayer from Cardiff, Wales

★

A whole world of love

350 Assurance of peace

To you, O God, we turn for peace ...

but grant us too the blessed assurance that nothing

shall deprive us of that peace, neither ourselves,

nor our foolish earthly desires, nor my wild

longings, nor the anxious cravings of my heart.

Søren Kierkegaard (1813–55), Denmark

351 Strength through kindness

They whose minds

are filled with kindness

will never enter

a world dark with woes.

No cruel wrongs

will ever overtake

anyone who protects

all living beings

and is kind to them.

Tiruvalluvar (c.500), India

352   The roots of our tears

Let your soul lend its ear to every cry of pain

as a lotus bares its heart to drink the morning sun.

Let not the fierce sun dry one tear of pain before

you yourself have wiped it from the sufferer's eye.

But let each burning human tear fall on your heart

and there remain, nor ever brush it off

until the pain that caused it is removed.

Traditional Vedic meditation

353   Variety

Unity in variety is the plan of the universe.

Vivekananda (1863–1902), India

354 In the service of all

The Lord of Love shines in the heart of all.

Seeing him in all creatures, the wise

Forget themselves in the service of all.

The Word is their joy, the Lord is their rest;

Such as they are the lovers of the Lord.

From the Mundaka Upanishad *(600–300BCE), India*

355 Lamps of love

O Lord, take my ears and hear through them,

take my hands and use them,

take my lips and speak through them,

take my eyes and smile through them,

take my heart and mind and will,

and use them as lamps of love,

by which your light may shine in all

the darkness of this suffering world.

Modern prayer, anonymous

356 The banquet

Love came, a guest

Within my breast.

My soul was spread,

Love banqueted.

Ibn Hazm (994–1064), Spain

357 Love's architecture

Believer is to fellow believer as parts

of a building which support each other.

Abu Musa, from an Islamic sacred text

358 Light through a gap

Light comes through a gap in the curtains:

the promise of morning.

Light comes through the flaws of our lives:

the promise of love.

Modern prayer from Berlin, Germany

359 With boundless mind

Even as a mother at the risk of her life would

watch over her only child, so let us with boundless

mind and goodwill survey the whole world.

The Buddha (c.563–c.483BCE), India

360 Unlimited love

Lord, may we love all your creation, all the Earth and every grain of sand in it. May we love every leaf, every ray of your light. For we acknowledge to you that all is like an ocean, all is flowing and blending, and that to withhold any measure of love from anything in your universe is to withhold that same measure from you.

Fyodor Dostoyevsky (1821–81), Russia

361 The extended family

I sought my soul

And the soul I could not see.

I sought my God

And God eluded me.

I sought my brother

And I found all three.

Modern prayer, anonymous

A universal language

362   Together in the heart

Pray not for Arab or Jew, for Palestinian or Israeli,

But pray rather for yourselves, that you may not divide

them in your prayers

But keep them both together in your hearts.

Christian prayer

363   The tree of being

All human beings powerfully sustain one another. The lovers
of God in this contingent world become the mercies and the
blessings sent out by that gentle King of the seen and unseen
realms. Let them purify their sight and behold all humankind
as leaves and blossoms and fruits of the Tree of Being.

Baha' Ullah (1817–1892), Persia

364 One God

As the rain dropping from the sky

wends its way toward the ocean,

So the prostrations offered in all faiths

reach the One God, who is supreme.

From the Rig Veda *(c.1500–c.1000BCE), India*

365 With one voice

In the adorations and benedictions of the righteous

The praises of all the prophets are kneaded together.

All their praises are mingled into one stream,

All the vessels are emptied into one ewer,

Because He that is praised is, in fact, only One.

In this respect all religions are only one religion,

Because all praises are directed toward God's light.

Jalil al-Din Rumi (1207–73), Persia

Index of first lines

Index of authors and sources

Acknowledgments

Acknowledgments have been listed by prayer number.

2 from TIDES AND SEASONS by David Adam, © SPCK, London, reprinted by kind permission of the copyright holders; **5, 269** from PRAYERS OF LIFE by Michel Quoist, reprinted by permission of Sheed and Ward, an Apostolate of the Priests of the Sacred Heart, 7373 S. Lovers Lane Rd, Franklin, WI 53132, and Gill & Macmillan, Dublin; **9, 39, 67, 83, 102** translated by Lucien Stryk, reproduced by kind permission of the translator; **14** "Litany" in CARIBBEAN VOICES, VOL. I: DREAMS AND VISIONS (Evans Brothers), reproduced by kind permission of George Campbell; **20** in ANOTHER DAY: PRAYERS OF THE HUMAN FAMILY, compiled and edited by John Carden, © SPCK, London, reprinted by kind permission of the copyright holders; **29** "Song for Fine Weather" in WORLD POETRY, 1928, edited by Mark van Doren, translated by Constance Lindsay Skinner; **31, 66, 82, 218, 288** from PRAYERS FOR A PLANETARY PILGRIM, compiled and edited by Edward Hays, © 1989, reprinted by kind permission of Forest of Peace Publishing, Inc, 251 Muncie Road, Leavenworth, KS 66048, USA; **33** in GOD OF A HUNDRED NAMES (Victor Gollancz Ltd) by Barbara Green and Victor Gollancz; **37** from THE ANGLICAN CHURCH OF KENYA HOLY COMMUNION LITURGY, reprinted by kind permission of the Most Rev. Dr David M. Gitari, Archbishop of Kenya and Bishop of Nairobi; **38** from MARKINGS by Dag Hammarskjöld, translated by Leif Sjoberg and W.H. Auden, reprinted by kind permission of Random House, Inc., New York and Faber and Faber Ltd, London; **42** in ONE HUNDRED WAYS TO SERENITY (Hodder and Stoughton), compiled by Celia Haddon, reprinted by kind permission of the Open Church Foundation, Box 81389, Wellesley Hills, Massachusetts 02481–0004; **43** from MORNING, NOON AND NIGHT, edited by John Carden, © Church Mission Society, London, 1967, reprinted by kind permission of the copyright holders; **44** © Gyldendal Norsk Forlag, 2001, translated by kind permission of the copyright holders, translation © Hanne Bewernick; **45, 70** in JAPANESE POETRY (Oxford University Press), translated by Arthur Waley, reprinted by kind permission of the Arthur Waley Estate; **58** from ECHO OF OUR SONG: CHANTS AND POEMS OF HAWAIIANS (University of Hawaii Press), translated by Kawena Pukui and Alfons L. Korn, © 1973, reprinted by kind permission of the publishers; **60** in WORLD POETRY (University of Hawaii Press), edited by Katherine Washburne and John S. Major, translated by Herbert J. Spinden; **74** in WOMEN IN PRAISE OF THE SACRED: FORTY-THREE CENTURIES OF SPIRITUAL POETRY BY WOMEN (HarperCollins*Publishers*, New York), edited by Jane Hirshfield, translated by Edwin W. Craston; **79** in LAUGHTER, SILENCE AND SHOUTING, AN ANTHOLOGY OF WOMEN'S PRAYERS (HarperCollins*Publishers*, London), edited by Kathy Keay, reprinted by kind permission of the publishers; **93** in WOMEN IN PRAISE OF THE SACRED: FORTY-THREE CENTURIES OF SPIRITUAL POETRY BY WOMEN (HarperCollins*Publishers*, New York), edited by Jane Hirshfield, translated by Gladys A. Reichard; **95** adaptation © Robert Saxton; **100** in THE GOLDEN THREAD by Dorothy Boux; **124, 173, 323** from JOURNEY FOR A SOUL (Collins, London), compiled and edited by George Appleton, © Rachel Bennett, reproduced by kind permission of the copyright holder; **126** from A RIVER RUNS THROUGH IT (University of Chicago Press) by Norman Maclean, 1976, reprinted by kind permission of the publishers; **132** from "Rubaiyat", from SELECTED POEMS (Carcanet Press Ltd) by Mimi Khalvati, © Mimi Khalvati 2000, reprinted by kind permission of the publishers; **138, 301** Rabindranath Tagore, © the Tagore Estate, Publishing Department, Visva-Bharati University, Calcutta; **139** from COLLECTED POEMS (Faber and Faber Ltd, London), © the MacNeice Estate, reprinted by permission of David Higham Associates, London; **150** from THE PALM AT THE END OF THE MIND by Wallace Stevens, edited by Holly Stevens, copyright © 1967, 1969, 1971 by Holly Stevens. Used by permission of Alfred A. Knopf, a division of Random House, Inc., and from COLLECTED POEMS (Faber and Faber Ltd, London), by Wallace Stevens, reprinted by kind permission of the publishers; **181** in EARTH AND SEASONS (HarperCollins*Publishers*, London), © through Marshall, Morgan & Scott; **183** in LALLA: NAKED SONGS (Maypop Books), translated by Coleman Barks, reprinted by kind permission of the translator; **210** in POETRY OF ASIA: FIVE MILLENNIA OF VERSE FROM THIRTY-THREE LANGUAGES, edited by Keith Bosley; **212, 307** from GITANJALI by Rabindranath Tagore, © the Tagore Estate, reprinted by kind permission of the Tagore Estate, Publishing Department, Visva-Bharati University, Calcutta; **223** Lady Izumi Shikibu, reprinted from TRADITIONAL JAPANESE POETRY: AN ANTHOLOGY, translated, with an Introduction, by Steven D. Carter, with the permission of the publishers, Stanford University Press, © 1991 by the Board of Trustees of the Leland Stanford Junior University; **228** in FORMS OF

PRAYER FOR JEWISH WORSHIP, VOLUME 1: DAILY AND SABBATH PRAYER BOOK, Reform Synagogues of Great Britain, London, 1977; **232** from EDGE OF GLORY: PRAYERS IN THE CELTIC TRADITION by David Adam, © SPCK, London, reprinted by kind permission of the copyright holders; **241** from WHY I AM NOT A CHRISTIAN by Bertrand Russell, first published by Allen & Unwin, © 1957, reprinted by kind permission of Routledge (Publishers); **247** from an ancient Welsh text, translated by Juliette Wood, reprinted by kind permission of the translator; **250** from THE NEW DAY BECKONS: PRAYERS BY SRI CHINMOY (Chinmoy Publications), © Sri Chinmoy 2001, reprinted by kind permission of the copyright holder; **258** "i thank You God for most this amazing" is reprinted from COMPLETE POEMS 1904–1962, by E.E. Cummings, edited by George J. Firmage, by permission of W.W. Norton & Company. Copyright © 1991 by the Trustees for the E.E. Cummings Trust and George James Firmage; **261** in the WISDOM OF THE EAST series, translated by Dulcie L. Smith, reprinted by permission of John Murray (Publishers) Ltd, London; **268** in ANOTHER DAY: PRAYERS OF THE HUMAN FAMILY, compiled and edited by John Carden, © SPCK, London, reprinted by kind permission of the coypyright holders; **290** in PRIVATE PRAYERS (Hodder and Stoughton); **300** from

THE PRAYERS OF KIRKEGAARD (University of Chicago Press) by Perry D. Lefevre, reprinted by kind permission of the publishers; **315** in GOD OF A HUNDRED NAMES (Victor Gollancz Ltd), by Barbara Green and Victor Gollancz; **329** from THE WEATHER IN JAPAN by Michael Longley, published by Jonathan Cape. Used by permission of The Random House Group Limited; **334** from NO CONTINUING CITY (Gill & Macmillan) by Michael Longley, © Michael Longley, reprinted by kind permission of Michael Longley; **348** from BIRDS OF HEAVEN (Phoenix House and Orion) by Ben Okri, reprinted by kind permission of the publishers and of David Godwin Associates, London.

The scripture quotations (**28, 63, 71, 78, 215, 259, 289**) contained herein are from the New Revised Standard Version Bible, copyright © 1989 by the Division of Christian Education of the National Council of the Churches of Christ in the USA, and are used by permission. All rights reserved.

The publishers have made every effort to contact copyright holders. We should like to apologize for any errors or omissions, which we will endeavor to rectify in any future editions of this book.

Photographic credits

The publisher would like to thank the following people and photographic libraries for permission to reproduce their material. Every care has been taken to trace copyright holders. However, if we have omitted anyone we apologise and will, if informed, make corrections in any future edition.

Images from Photonica, London appear on pages **6** William Self; **7** T. Shinoda; **8–9** Alan Shirulniko; **10** Steven Edson; **12** S. Tokitsune; **14–5**; **16** Mia Klein; **18** Liam Bailey; **20–1** Richard Glover; **23** L'aura Colan; **25** Erik Rank; **26** S. Yoshimori; **28** Carlos Seechin; **30–1** Dick Lauria; **33** F. Villaflor; **34–5** Joe Squillant; **36** Edgar Lissel; **38–9** Akira Inoue; **40** B. Schmid; **42** Schoichi; **44** Elaine Mayers; **46** Kaz Chiba; **51** Masao Ota; **53** Charles Gulling; **54–5**; **56** Doug Plummer; **58–9** Bildhuset AB; **60** S. Eguchi; **62** B. Schmid; **64** Stuart Simons; **67** Steven Edson; **68–9** Nick David; **70** Shooting Star; **72** Toshiya Kumakura; **74–5** Ryuicho Sato; **77** Starrex; **84** H. Sakuramoto; **87** Yusuke Yoshino; **89** Brian McWeeney; **90** D. Brookover; **92** Minori Kawana; **94** Y. Kanazawa; **97** Yoichi Nagata; **100–1** William Huber;

102 Bildhuset AB; **105** Keyvan Behpour; **107** Steven Edson; **108** Barnaby Hall; **111** William Self; **112–3** Francesca Sims; **114** Alan Montaigne; **117**; **119** Makoto Takada; **122** Takuya Inokuma; **124–5** Akira Inoue; **127** Paul Vozdic; **128** Doug Plummer; **130** Kazumi Nagasawa; **132–3** R. Murakami; **135** Chery Koralic; **136** Paul Griggs; **139** G. Kloppenburg; **140–1** H. Okamoto; **142–3** Andy Katz; **144–5** Michael Darter; **146** Doug Plummer; **148–9** Yutaka Iijima; **150** Peter Murphy; **152–3** B. Schmid; **157** Mel Curtis; **158** T. Yamaguchi; **160** Jake Wyman; **162–3** Doug Plummer; **166** Bengt Olof Olss; **168** Tommy Flynn; **170** William Self; **177** Keyvan Behpour; **178–9** Yusuke Yoshino; **182–3** Alex Maclean; **184** T. Sasaki; **186** Jim Friendman; **189** Ron Rovtar; **190** William Self; **193** Doug Plummer; **194–5** Yutaka Iijima; **198** Naoki Mutai; **202** K. Hashimoto; **205** Jonathan Safir; **206–7**; **208** F. Villaflor; **211** Starrex; **213** Hiroshi Hara; All images from National Geographic/Images Colour Library appear on pages **120–1**, **197** and **214–5**. Images from Tony Stone/Getty Images appear on pages **48**, **80**, **155**, **164–5**, **172** and **174**.